TIBET

As an award-winning chef, **Günter Hager**, who was born in Austria's Salzkammergut region, organised 'International Austrian Gourmet Weeks' in faraway Asia in the 1980s. In 1998, he crossed the Himalayas out of a sheer sense of adventure. What he did not know at the time was that he was laying the foundations for a deep friendship with the Tibetan people. Today, the passionate restaurateur successfully runs a traditional inn in the Upper Austrian capital of Linz. Yet for more than a quarter of a century, Günter Hager has always found time to visit and explore the Tibetan side of northern India. z

A close connection to this maltreated people, which has grown steadily over the decades, has now led to his very personal credo: 'If there is such a thing as reincarnation, then I myself was once one of them in a previous life.' His new book focuses on his long-standing friendships with Buddhist monks, old mountain nomads and the Tibetan children who escaped from his orphanages. But they are crowned by impressive experiences of his numerous encounters with His Holiness the Dalai Lama. Günter Hager's utterly authentic stories provide an almost intimate insight into a world we know little about, and a way of life very different from that of Western culture. They are a worthy continuation of the work of previous great Austrian Tibet researchers such as Johann Grueber, Herbert Tichy and Heinrich Harrer.

TIBET
WHERE HAPPINESS IS AT HOME

GÜNTER HAGER

Om Books International

First published in 2025 by

Om Books International

Corporate & Editorial Office
A-12, Sector 64, Noida 201 301
Uttar Pradesh, India
Phone: +91 120 477 4100
Email: editorial@ombooks.com
Website: www.ombooksinternational.com

Sales Office
107, Ansari Road, Darya Ganj,
New Delhi 110 002, India
Phone: +91 11 4000 9000
Email: sales@ombooks.com
Website: www.ombooks.com

Copyright © Günter Hager 2025

ALL RIGHTS RESERVED. The views and opinions expressed in this book are those of the author, and have been verified to the extent possible, and the publishers are in no way liable for the same. No part of this book may be reproduced or transmitted in any form by any means, electronic or mechanical, including photocopying and recording, or by any information storage and retrieval system, except as may be expressly permitted in writing by the publisher.

ISBN: 978-93-63952-53-9

Printed in India

10 9 8 7 6 5 4 3 2 1

Contents

Foreword by the Dalai Lama	vii
Preface	ix
Prologue: How It All Began (1998 Tour)	xi
1. Icons of Peace: A Chance Meeting	1
2. Preparing for the Journey	5
3. Dangerous Indian Roads	11
4. At the Tibetan Thangka Painting School	16
5. At the Corpse Pass	24
6. First Meeting with the Dalai Lama	34
7. Jakob in the Mountains	39
8. At the Tibetan Children's Villages	45
9. The Himalayas Are Burning!	56
10. My First Audience	65
11. The Concert in the Himalayas	71
12. The Tibetan Waiter	85
13. The Opening of the Temple	93
14. Inside the Cave of Padmasambhava	106

15. At Home in Dharamshala	113
16. 'Amala': The Mother of Tibet	119
17. 'Ibiza Boy' or the Spanish Reincarnation	125
18. Managers in the Himalayas	133
19. Watching the Dalai Lama Teach	158
20. Opening of Home Josef 2	167
21. Meeting the God of Love	175
22. My Friend, the Maharaja	186
23. St John in the Wilderness	197
24. Died of Heartbreak	203
25. Shots Fired in the Himalayas	210
Epilogue: Between Dream and Reality:	
A Tibetan Fairy Tale	214
Glossary	231
Acknowledgements	235

THE DALAI LAMA

FOREWORD

I am pleased to see that Gunter Hager, a dedicated supporter of the Tibetan people has written about his experience of years of interaction with the Tibetan community in exile.

Providing a holistic education to the Tibetan refugee children has been our main focus and it is individuals like Mr. Hager, who stepped forward in supporting our effort by providing material and moral support. Through his several visits to the Tibetan schools in India he has also become aware of the contribution that the Tibetan culture and tradition can make to this world.

I thank Mr. Hager for his support and his initiative in bringing out this book, *Tibet*. I am sure the readers will find it beneficial.

With my prayers.

13 February 2019

Preface

The story I am about to share is my own. It is the story of my adventures and experiences hundreds of kilometres from home. It is the story of people I have met on my travels and of the impressions that have made me the person I am today. Hours of happiness, moments of reflection, joy and sadness—they make up the sum of the footprints I will leave behind in the great journey of life.

And yet it seems to me that all this is just a small part of a mysterious karma; invisible ties that wondrously connect two distant worlds and cultures; fates that ensure that these differences meet again and again over the centuries. It is a crossroads of two such disparate worlds, the multiple meanings of which we humans will never fully understand. Perhaps there is something in the Buddhist faith that redefines the meaning of life. But what exactly is it? What triggers this longing for the unknown, which at the same time seems so familiar? My life will not be long enough to explore this.

Great sons of my homeland followed their karma and became sons of the Himalayas. Who doesn't know them? Herbert Tichy, Heinrich Harrer, Peter Aufschnaiter and

Hermann Gmeiner, the founders of the SOS Children's Villages. And yet they were not the first to undertake arduous and eventful journeys to these distant lands, and I too feel a deep connection with them.

Long before them, the Franciscan monk Odoric von Portenau from Pordenone in northern Italy and the Jesuit priest Johann Grueber from Linz—on their own and for different reasons—had set out centuries earlier on long-distance journeys to China, Tibet, India, Goa, Mongolia and many other far-flung destinations.

I will dedicate the end of my story to all of them, for it was their adventures that inspired and motivated me to explore these seemingly foreign worlds, and last but not least, made me write these lines.

Prologue

How It All Began (1998 Tour)

Between lush meadows dotted with cattle, the glittering waters of the Achensee, only seemingly encircled by the mighty peaks of the Karwendel mountain range, generations of a hard-working and industrious family had built one of the most beautiful alpine hotels in the Tyrolean mountains. It had everything, from spacious wellness facilities, saunas and steam baths to saltwater pools. Award-winning chefs, a uniquely stocked wine cellar and young, friendly waitresses were the reasons why we repeatedly took time out from the hectic lives of a family of restaurateurs.

Over the years, we developed a close friendship with Karl, the owner of this temple of luxury relaxation in the middle of the mountains. It was not uncommon for us to sit together for hours, even at night, talking about the wonderful but tough profession we had both chosen, about the restrictions and hurdles that we restaurateurs face, the worries and hardships everyone who works in the industry knows. And it wasn't unusual for us to exchange odd anecdotes about guests and staff. I quickly realised that Karl and I were cut from the same cloth. And I noticed his interest even more when I told him about my time abroad in Beijing and Hong Kong, where I was head chef at the Austrian Gastronomy Weeks.

My choice of career as a chef was preceded by an endless desire to travel far and wide. Unfortunately, friendships, relationships, professional commitments and my training with great celebrity chefs had repeatedly prevented me from satisfying my burning desire to travel in the big, wide world. However, guest appearances lasting several weeks allowed me to learn about many Asian cultures and their people.

Now, however, I was the proud owner of Linz's first award-winning restaurant. I was fully committed to my guests and the development of a new culinary philosophy, 'nouvelle cuisine'.

Conversations with Karl were like balm on the wounds you inevitably inflict on yourself along the way. And Karl was an intelligent, attentive listener, always ready to offer advice. Had he been born in another century, he would certainly have ranked among the great Asian scholars such as Confucius or Lao Tzu. I admired him. I often secretly wrote down his philosophical statements, so that I could look them up later. He was not a tall, powerful figure, but rather small, almost delicately built. Long, thin blond hair fell over his shoulders, and his aura and great kindness were incomparable and impressive. We used to talk about our great dream to travel to Lhasa, the mysterious capital of Tibet, in the Himalayas.

One day, it was time. During a phone call, I asked Karl if he would like to join me on a trip to our dream country. I felt it had to be now. I didn't want to wait any longer. For a moment there was silence. Karl was probably busy with one of his many guests and I immediately realised how inappropriate my call was. But after those few seconds, which seemed like hours then, I heard a 'yes'. And then, as if we were talking about a little hike, he said, 'I'll join you in Zurich.'

Nothing stood in the way of our trip. I was a master planner. I had already devoured books upon books, all the contacts of Austrian friends in China had been used and informed. In the end, everyone knew we were coming!

Vienna–Zurich–Beijing was the flight route. I had been to China several times during catering weeks, and had made many friends in the hotel and business sectors in Beijing. One such friend was Mr Shue, a Chinese stock market guru from Hunan. I had met him through Franz, an old chef colleague and a long-time friend.

One day, Franz came to me with a very special request. Mr Shue's son was one of the many Chinese piano prodigies—a little 'Lang Lang', so to speak. He had already given concerts in many major cities around the world. But his greatest wish was to be a guest at the Vienna Philharmonic's New Year's Concert. It was almost impossible for his father to get a ticket—the concerts are usually sold out years in advance. This was the reason behind his call: he was requesting me to find a ticket.

Even then, the catering network was something special. I managed to get the boy one of the coveted tickets for the New Year's concert relatively quickly.

When Mr Shue heard about our short stay in the capital of the Chinese empire, he invited us to one of his many luxury restaurants. Of course, we accepted.

Rarely had we seen so much pomp, circumstance and glamour in one place. We enjoyed the highlights of classic Chinese cuisine. We ate from gold plates with gold cutlery and sat on original Versace sofas. Mr Shue proudly told us that his chef had cooked for the last emperor. She was one of the last in her profession to master the art of imperial Chinese cuisine.

This was served with a great French Bordeaux from the best vintage in large magnum bottles. Unfortunately, this was not poured into the finely cut wine glasses provided. The fine wine simply ended up in water glasses. When Mr Shue mixed his vintage Bordeaux with classic Coca-Cola, we found it difficult to keep our composure. Karl and I looked at each other and chuckled. Money and wealth are no substitute for the art of pleasure. As is still the case today, this great Chinese hospitality was mixed with international capitalist megalomania.

We stayed with the representative of Voestalpine, one of Austria's largest steel companies. Gerhard was married to a Chinese woman called Madeleine. We were always grateful that she acted as our interpreter. Madeleine gave us the opportunity to get to know Beijing away from the tourist crowds. I will never forget the Austrian welcome party she organised, on a tower of the mighty Great Wall of China, far from the gates of Beijing.

We drank Austria's finest Schlumberger sparkling wine as an aperitif and red wine from our favourite winemaker, Ernst Triebaumer, with crispy Wiener schnitzel. And the general manager of Beijing's Holiday Inn, Jimmy, who hailed from the Waldviertel region, served us an original Austrian Gugelhupf with our coffee. What would the great Chinese emperors have said about this feast?

The farewell party (all within a few days) was no less original. Just outside Beijing, Gerhard and his wife had organised a barbecue in one of the thirteen Ming tombs. In front of a fifteenth-century backdrop, we enjoyed the Käsekrainer we had brought from Linz's master butcher Lackinger, while a Kung Fu film was being made in the immediate vicinity of the tomb. What an experience!

Unfortunately, I was not able to visit the tomb again during my many subsequent visits. It makes sense that this piece of ancient Chinese culture has simply been fenced off with barbed wire—no trespassing!

Next Destination: Xi'an

An old friend and fellow Austrian chef working in Beijing had asked one of his Chinese chefs, who had just spent his home leave in Xi'an, to show us his hometown. After almost twenty-four hours on the train, Chang was waiting for us at the station to take us to the hotel.

I had heard a lot about Xi'an, this legendary, mystical city. For a long time, it was the capital of the Chinese empire, and the centre is still surrounded by mighty city walls. During one of my morning walks, I spent several hours walking around it. Xi'an was the city of the most powerful of all Chinese emperors. It was under his reign that Qin Shi Huang united the warring empires in 221 BC. He was known as a cruel and strict leader. To this day, his tomb is sealed under a huge mound of earth and many mysteries surround its interior. However, the tomb housing the huge army that was to accompany the ruler on his journey after death has already been opened. Words such as 'impressive', 'significant', 'unique' or any other glorifying attributes that come to mind will never be enough to adequately describe the Terracotta Army that is now known throughout the world. It is not for nothing that it is the main reason why millions of visitors from all over the world make the pilgrimage to the place every year.

The Terracotta Army was also the absolute highlight for us. The mysterious warriors of Qin Shi Huang stand silently in rank and file, as if still waiting for their emperor's order to deploy. As a big Bruce Lee karate fan, I remembered that not far from there was the legendary Shaolin Monastery, a place of pilgrimage for many martial artists. Oh, how I would have loved to make a short detour there!

With Chang, we couldn't have asked for a better guide. He showed us the city he grew up in as he knew it. We wandered through narrow alleyways, climbed the Giant Wild Goose Pagoda and felt like imperial warriors walking along the fortress wall under attack from enemy hordes. We visited the first Chinese swimming pools, carved in stone, and dreamed of the Chinese playmates who would have bathed here in front of their rulers, scantily clad.

Later we tried to fathom the art of noodle-making, which is characterised by the fact that no knife is used in its making, owing to a folding system that was incomprehensible to us. Although Chang tried very hard to teach us this technique, our attempts failed miserably. While Italians are known as the inventors of pasta, noodles was being made in China in hundreds of variations since hundreds of years before Christ.

To say goodbye, Chang invited us to an unusual restaurant with an unusual speciality: a snake dinner. With a queasy feeling in our stomachs, we took his advice and chose the 'five-step snake'! A very strange name indeed. It took Chang's explanation to help us make sense of it: No one would be able to walk more than five steps after being bitten by this creature, he told us.

At the entrance to the hut, which was called a restaurant, there were iron cages in which various species of these crawling reptiles were kept. Chang pondered for a moment and then pointed to a two-metre-long 'monster' that the waiter was holding from its head using iron tongs. I walked in the opposite direction (these creatures frighten me). By the time I returned, the waiter had already cut off the snake's head with iron scissors. Now they were collecting the blood in a Chinese liquor container by lifting the dead snake's tail.

The heart and liver of the snake are considered a special gift for the guest of honour. The skin is peeled off and the snake is cut into pieces. During the subsequent visit to the rather dirty kitchen, I learned the secrets of preparation, but I still quite didn't understand some aspects of it.

We sat down at the round table in the restaurant and, for the first time, I regretted being the 'guest of honour'. I was ceremoniously served the still-beating heart and liver of the crawling creature in lukewarm Chinese liquor in a porcelain bowl. I would rather not describe my taste experience in detail. Yes, I ate both innards, and no, I did not gain any of the supposed aphrodisiac insights from them. The soup served with the snake parts tasted like clear chicken soup, so it was very good. But the fried skin of the reptile tasted more like sushi—and that was not good.

Karl and I were already thinking about the next day's main stage, the journey to Lhasa, the mysterious capital of Tibet. To avoid any more similar 'guest of honour dinners', we went to a Chinese supermarket to buy the necessary food. After all of that, we stocked up on food as if we were going on an expedition that would last several weeks. The food was very cheap, but unfortunately, we hadn't reckoned with the strict Chinese checks at the airport the next day—with every kilo charged as expensive excess baggage, we could have afforded a dinner on golden plates in Lhasa similar to the one we had seen in Beijing.

Lhasa, the Capital of the Dalai Lama

Sitting in the plane, we looked out over the vastness of the Tibetan Plateau below us— an imposing, infinitely flat expanse, rightly called the 'roof of the world'. Countless thoughts flashed through my mind. The countless mystical stories and tales of Tibet's impressive culture that have inspired me for years came rushing back to me. Every time I think about it, I am overcome with helpless rage. The Tibetans are an oppressed people. Thousands of monasteries were blown up and razed to the ground by the People's Liberation Army of China after it invaded the mountainous country in the late 1950s. But what are the Chinese doing there? There is nothing but mountain peaks rising steeply into the sky, almost impossible to conquer. All I see is sand and desert. An endless, barren area; no trees, no lush meadows, no fields. Mineral resources? Not a thing! The conquest of Tibet by the Chinese rulers was based on one single reason, the most reprehensible of all: its unique strategic location in relation to its arch-enemy India.

However, China has learnt a lesson, and its conquests now differ from those of America. It is no longer invading with the military, tanks and soldiers as it did in Tibet in the past, but quietly and secretly infiltrating desirable countries and cultures with the now-indispensable Chinese economy. No president or head of state in the West dares to jeopardise their economic dependence on China. On the contrary, they are cautiously, almost meekly, accepting the increasingly harsh tone coming from Beijing.

China already owns vast tracts of fertile land in Africa to feed the increasingly important 1.4 billion hungry Chinese. Mines, airports and ports in Africa, South America and Europe have long been snapped up by far-sighted Chinese managers.

The Chinese juggernaut thinks in terms of generations, whereas in our Western latitudes, politics usually limits its 'survival cycle' to a more or less long period of government. Necessary decisions by our governments have become increasingly cumbersome and are often short-lived, as they can always be overturned by a potential successor, according to the laws of our democracies. A largely misunderstood democracy, prosperity, bureaucracy, and then the evermore cumbersome political decisions required as a result are the heavy menhir of the West, while in an authoritarian state like China, the rulers have every conceivable means of extending their power first in their own country and then around the world.

Is this the 'yellow peril' that Nostradamus had warned about at the turn of the millennium? Covid-19 may have been the most impressive diversionary tactic in this case. China's dictatorship allowed its economy to do business around the world, while Western entrepreneurs had to hide in coronavirus lockdown. In my view, however, the supply shortages during the pandemic were the harbingers of a clever Chinese economic strategy.

After a more or less successful military operation, the US still tries to boost the business of American companies in the countries it occupies, so that they can land billions of dollars' worth of deals, although this usually ends in unsuccessful reconstruction. The ruins of war are quickly joined by the ruins of a failed economy, along with angry and utterly impoverished citizens.

China's approach has been much more subtle and successful. With far-sighted foresight, Confucian chairs have already been installed in more than 170 universities around the world, skilfully infiltrating the traditional culture of these countries.

Anyone with a passing knowledge of Chinese history knows about the Opium War. The British Empire made the whole of China dependent on it and reaped huge economic benefits. This time it will probably be the other way round.

I was still deep in thought when we finally landed at one of the highest airports in the world: Lhasa Gonggar Airport at an incredible 3,570 metres above sea level.

Karl and I were curious to see if and how the unusually thin air would affect us. The professionals were slowly getting used to the altitude. We were more interested in 'learning by doing': 'Let's see how we feel.' Most of the time it worked. But our method is not really recommended for copying.

During that visit in the mid-1990s, I heard about the idea of connecting this airport with the city of Lhasa, just a few kilometres away, by rail. Given the almost impassable, rugged terrain, it sounded ambitious, if not crazy. But today, some thirty years later, that short link is history, replaced by the legendary overland railway connecting China's far-flung metropolises.

Comfortable and equipped with all the modern conveniences, these trains are packed with Chinese tourists, often for months on end. It is terrible how the railway lines have destroyed the unique image of the lonely mountain landscapes. Not only do they disrupt the traditional migrations of the wild animals that live in such great diversity but also upset the ecological system. At the same time, China's tourist marketing machine is creating a strangely unreal fantasy world that is mercilessly drowning out the once peaceful aura of many Buddhist places of worship. As a result, many traditions and ancient values are sadly being lost.

Chinese airport architecture, made of loveless concrete, greeted us with an icy cold wind and we gasped for air like pond carp fished out of the water. We were glad to get into one of those old, rattling Chinese taxis. We were now ready for Lhasa!

Ernst, a good friend from Stadl-Paura in Upper Austria, had reserved rooms for us at the Holiday Inn. Ernst was a hotel pioneer in Asia. He had built this hotel in Lhasa years ago as general manager of the American hotel group, together with the Chinese occupying forces.

I still remember his endless stories of the weeks of negotiations with Chinese party politicians in Lhasa. A lot of mao-tai, Chinese liquor, had to be consumed before permission was finally granted to build this hotel.

In the early days, the hotel was run by an Austrian. Like many others up here, he died of an unknown disease. Whatever it was, we Europeans cannot thrive in such altitude for long—Karl and I were no exceptions. Exhausted, we fell into our beds in the uncharming rooms of the hotel, always thinking of the oxygen bottles on our bedside tables.

The long journey, the flight and the thin air let us sink into a wonderful dream. I dreamed blissfully of the first Miss Tibet contest, which had been held in this hotel years ago and which Ernst had told me about many times.

A particularly creative director had come up with the idea of a beauty pageant to increase the hotel's footfall. Journalists from Hong Kong and Beijing were invited to cover the event. In principle, it was a good marketing strategy.

In reality, things turned out a little differently. Weeks before the idea was conceived, the hotel was plagued by a huge infestation of rats. As more and more guests complained about the grey, ugly creatures, rat poison was flown in from Hong Kong and laid out. To be on the safe side, the predominantly Tibetan staff were told that the blue pellets were not to be eaten but were only to be used as a powerful poison to kill the rats. It didn't take long for the blue pellets to take effect.

At the same time, the hotel's thrifty manager had turned down the heating due to low occupancy to save precious energy. Though this made sense, it also meant that hundreds of poisoned dead rodents were now being kept cool in the hotel's ventilation ducts, false floors and wooden ceilings.

Finally, the eagerly awaited day of the Miss Tibet pageant arrived. It hadn't been easy to persuade the fifteen or so Tibetan girls to wear their national costumes on the hotel's makeshift ramp. Bathing costumes, or even bikinis that showed bare skin, were strictly forbidden by the Chinese authorities, and it was doubtful that the Tibetan girls would have been persuaded to appear in such unusual attire.

In any case, the event fell far short of the rather voyeuristic expectations of the press and local celebrities who had flown in. Their modest applause for the lavishly organised event was limited.

Suddenly, it was the freezing cold that drew the most criticism. The hotel manager, who was always keen to make sure his guests were warm and comfortable, had a simple solution. He turned the heating up to full power.

However, no one had thought about the rat carcasses in the ventilation ducts, which were thawed out by the sudden heat and emitted a terrible smell. Unfortunately, the reaction of the press was not as expected.

I woke up from my idiosyncratic dream to find my friend Karl already packing his travel gear into the boxes. It was time to visit our destination.

We had seen the stunning backdrop of the Potala Palace—probably the largest and most imposing palace in Buddhist culture—far too many times in books and films. Now it was time to come face to face with the magnificent dwelling of the lamas—the ultimate goal of our journey.

But something was bothering me about this wonderful image that had been so firmly imprinted on my mind. On the way to the Potala Palace, we crossed cobbled streets with the usual Chinese street lamps. What didn't fit into this harmonious picture was the military. Military as far as the eye could see. Images of the occupying forces after the Second World War immediately came to mind. Yes, it must have been like that when the Americans, Soviets, British and French drove through our occupied Vienna.

I felt a sense of fear rising in me. We were being watched very closely. European long-noses were seldom guests here—we could be taken for spies.

Now I noticed the machine guns of the soldiers. The uniformed men stood heavily armed behind sandbags. Large-calibre machine guns were also positioned at the main road junctions. I could feel the mistrust of the soldiers. They were all occupiers, warriors of a foreign army in a country that only recently had defended itself with simple weapons, including bows and arrows, against powerful and modern armed invaders.

Surrounded by the highest mountains in the world, endless hot deserts and icy glaciers, it would have been easy to deny foreigners access to this mysterious land. But by sealing itself off from other territories, it also failed to modernise its traditional defences. The Buddhist belief in the 'goodness of man' alone was of little help against the invasion of hundreds of thousands of Chinese soldiers who occupied this vast country in the 1950s on the pretext that it had been part of the Chinese empire for centuries.

I am aware that lines like these will prevent my book from ever being distributed and read in China. After all, I am about to become an enemy of the state by writing this text.

It is difficult for a person born in a Western democracy to understand that he is not allowed to express his free opinion. Like Hollywood star Richard Gere, a long-time friend of the Dalai Lama, I will probably never be allowed to enter the Land of the Yellow Dragon again. So be it. If something similar happens to me, I will do what Richard Gere did and consider it a special honour for my contribution to the ongoing struggle for the freedom of my Tibetan friends.

Then it finally hit me. All the tourist pictures and photos I had seen of Lhasa were deliberately taken to show only the beauty, mystery and awe of this historic city. It was all fake, nothing less than a scam for tourists! A deliberate strategy had been adopted to ensure that the almost eerily negative energy emanating from the heavily armed Chinese soldiers, military jeeps and police officers could not be detected. The outside world was made to believe that everything was absolutely perfect. Anyone who saw these photos would have been impressed. On the ground, I could feel the crackling danger and fear experienced by the locals with my eyes closed.

It sent shivers down my spine. I thought I was in a surreal war film. My dream of finally seeing and experiencing this mysterious, peaceful pilgrimage site of Buddhist culture shattered into a thousand pieces. For centuries, it had been forbidden for foreigners to visit this city, hidden for generations behind the high peaks of the Himalayas, at the end of the world. Only a few had been able to enter the country. For me, it was both a blessing and a curse—I had arrived years too late. Soon, more hopeless uprisings by the natives would be brutally crushed by the occupying forces. A spiritual science so important to all of humanity is being eradicated and 'rebuked'. China has something that other conquerors do not have: money, military power and, above all, a lot of time.

I had read so many books about this mysterious jewel, Tibet. The countless stories of the Austrian Heinrich Harrer, who was the Dalai Lama's personal teacher and a very special friend of His Holiness until his death.

In this context, I think it is worth mentioning that the first European recorded in history to have seen the Potala Palace in Lhasa in the seventeenth century was also an Austrian, indeed from my hometown of Linz. The Jesuit priest Johann Grueber spent about four weeks there in 1661. The 'great' fifth Dalai Lama, Ngawang Lobsang Gyatso, one of the most famous Lama in the history of the fourteen Dalai lamas, began building the Potala Palace at that time. Unfortunately, we do not know if he met Grueber in person. It is possible that his Jesuit pride did not allow him to pay his respects to such a great 'competitor in faith'. But the fact remains that Grueber was here in Lhasa on his way from Beijing via Nepal to Goa and Agra on his way back to his native land, Austria. Grueber was travelling on behalf of the Pope to find the overland route from China to Europe, becoming the first European to do so.

Johann Grueber: Jesuit Priest and Globetrotter

'To the memory of the famous explorer, born in Linz on 28 October 1623; 1659 to '61, court astronomer in Peking, on journeys through China, Tibet, India and Persia, died on 30 September 1680 in Sárospatak/ Hungary': the inscription on a memorial plaque in front of the Freinberg Church in Linz sounds fascinating. But who was this 'Linzer Entdeckerreisende' (Linz explorer), who is hardly known today? The answer to this question reveals the story about an incredible life.

Johann Grueber first attended the Jesuit grammar school Aloisianum in Linz and, after further studies in Vienna, Leoben and four years of theological studies in Graz, he was ordained a priest in 1655.

A year later, he and his brother Bernhard Diestel were chosen for a very special mission. They were commissioned by the Pope to explore a land route to China.

Travelling via Venice, the eastern Mediterranean and Smyrna, they reached Isfahan in Persia in 1656. The dangerous turmoil of war prevented them from continuing their journey across Asia. The only option left was the sea route to India. Unfortunately, they had little luck there. When they arrived in Velha Goa, the city then known as the 'Rome of the Orient', they were summarily arrested by the authorities. It was ten months before they regained their freedom, and in July 1658 a merchant ship took them to the Portuguese colony of Macau. It was only a stopover, but the arduous journey till there had already taken two years.

The onward journey to Beijing was more difficult than planned. It was strictly forbidden for non-believers to enter the city. Nevertheless, Grueber and Diestel persevered, and their perseverance was rewarded when, in April 1659, they received permission to continue their journey to the 'Forbidden City' of Peking. On 22 April 1659, the vice-provincial Simon da Cunha issued the official order that they should go to Peking and then explore the land route in the opposite direction. It must have been a moment of triumph: Diestel and Grueber were escorted to Peking at state expense.

Grueber spent the next two years at the imperial court. As the court astronomer and draughtsman, he quickly found a close confidant in the German Jesuit Johann Adam Schall von Bell. He had already been appointed director of the Imperial Astronomical Office at the Chinese court.

After the demise of Diestel, who could not tolerate the climate in Peking from the outset, on 13 September 1660, Grueber returned to

Europe by land seven months later, in April 1661, together with the Belgian Jesuit Albert d'Orville.

They left Chinese territory via Xinan and Xining in mid-July 1661 and travelled in a caravan in a south-westerly direction along the shores of Qinghai Lake, crossing the Tibetan highlands north of Lhasa and finally reaching the Tibetan capital of Lhasa via the Trans-Himalayas on 6 October 1661, becoming the first Europeans ever to do so.

During his four-week stay, Grueber made numerous drawings. The pictures of the Potala Palace were probably the first faithful depictions of this monumental building in Europe. The same goes for the depictions of Far Eastern prayer wheels, religious monuments and, in particular, a portrait of the Fifth Dalai Lama, Ngawang Lobsang Gyatso, based on a painting at the entrance to the palace. Grueber was not able to see the Dalai Lama himself. As a Catholic priest, he did not want to submit to the prescribed ceremonies.

Although Grueber repeatedly stressed the many 'similarities' between Buddhism and the Catholic Church as remarkable, he felt that it could only be a 'work of the devil'. Reason: 'because no European or Christian has ever been there'.

No, he could not and did not tolerate the Buddhist faith. This is shown by a quote from Grueber's letters about his time in Lhasa: 'We have seen wonderful things ... and there is justified hope for the conversion of these peoples ... indeed, if that diabolical God the Father in the Potala had not decreed that anyone who does not worship him should be punished immediately with death.'

The current Dalai Lama summarised a fallacy during a visit to Salzburg in response to a question on the subject: 'There is actually no difference worth mentioning, neither religion knows its boss, only the Catholic Church has slightly more bosses.'

Despite the snow and ice, Grueber and d'Orville began their journey home in September 1662. They crossed the Himalayas in winter, Nepal at the end of the year and, after further stops in Patna and Benares, finally arrived in Agra, the residence of the Indian Grand Mogul Shah Jahan, at the end of March 1662.

Grueber was probably not only the first European to see the famous Potala Palace but also one of the first Europeans to admire the Taj Mahal shortly after its completion.

He continued on his return journey. Together with d'Orville, he left Agra on 4 September 1662. The two missionaries made their way back to Europe overland via Kabul, Persia and Asia Minor, arriving in Rome on 20 February 1664.

His detailed and—for the time—sensational travel reports were so well received that the polymath Athanasius Kircher included them in his famous *Encyclopaedia China Illustrata* in 1667. There is no doubt that Johann Grueber was an exceptional and courageous man, a 'primus inter pares' who should not be forgotten, at least by the citizens of Linz!

Now I was finally in Lhasa. I had been dreaming of it for years. But the city was swarming with soldiers and secret police. An icy aura of unfriendliness and suspicion wafted towards us. No, it is no longer Tibet with its kind and friendly people. The seeds of evil are growing there. The argument of the Chinese occupying forces that 'Tibet has always belonged to China' has been arbitrary. If it were universally valid, almost any state in the world could act accordingly and annex small neighbouring countries without further ado. Yes, there have always been historical border shifts. But the pervasive violence and fear we were confronted with made this argument absurd. Forcible annexation against the will of an entire people is inhumane. It must not be allowed.

Karl was no better off. We made the best of what was an arduous journey. Tsering, our Tibetan driver, had lived with this fear since birth. He was the one who tried to change this perception a little.

With him, we visited the Jokang, the oldest Buddhist temple. Of course, we passed the omnipresent Chinese soldiers. But it was still impressive. There we saw Tibetan pilgrims praying by throwing themselves to the ground hundreds of times in a dignified posture with folded hands, hoping to achieve nirvana sooner. Old Tibetans, with faces furrowed by the icy wind, turned their prayer wheels and murmured the mantra '*Om mani padme hum*'[1] with an absent-minded serenity and an enviable ignorance of Mao's warriors.

I almost smiled. Perseverance, charity and consistency in their non-violent struggle for faith have always characterised these mysterious people. We could learn so much from them. If only we wanted to.

Nowhere in the world is there anything negative that does not bring something positive with it. It is the famous yin and yang. It was Tibetan Buddhism, the seeds of which were carried across the world by the children who fled the oppression that gave us the incredible good fortune to be able to learn this wonderful philosophy of life: happiness and sadness coexist.

The three days of sightseeing in Lhasa passed quickly and without much emotion. We learned that in addition to the 150,000 or so Tibetans, 200,000 Chinese soldiers and newly resettled Chinese from all parts of the vast empire were already living in Lhasa. The sixty-five discos were supposed to entertain occupiers and visitors. Prostitution, alcohol and bribery were the order of the day. No, this was not the world we were looking for.

---

1 In dependence on the practice of a path which is an indivisible union of method and wisdom, you can transform your impure body, speech and mind into the pure exalted body, speech and mind of a Buddha.

The three great monasteries of Sera, Drepung and Ganden were a different story. We were particularly impressed by Ganden. Situated high in the mountains, it was home to around 20,000 monks in its heyday. After the People's Liberation Army (PLA) of China invaded the place, it was levelled with tonnes of dynamite. Tibetan prisoners were made to clear the rubble after the demolition. This was done to prevent the rebuilding of the temple. However, the Chinese government soon realised that these old monasteries can attract tourists into the country and bring in a lot of money. So they spent a lot of money rebuilding Ganden. However, this has not brought back much of the Buddhist flair. You can't miss the many soldiers. They charge a hefty entrance fee and make sure that the monks have as little contact with the tourists as possible.

Tsering drove his jeep to the hotel early in the morning. We loaded our luggage and set off across the Tibetan highlands to Kathmandu. It was going to be an exciting journey—past Gyantse and Shigatse and the Himalayan Base Camp. Past the turn-off to Lake Manasarovar and the holy Mount Kailash, the many jeeps on our roads, with countless tourists from the distant metropolises of China, slowly took away my desire to visit these sacred Buddhist sites one day.

I have travelled to China and visited its sights several times and I am still a great admirer of its culture. Maybe I feel like the Dalai Lama. He once said to me in conversation: 'I have nothing against the Chinese people, but I have something against the Chinese government!'

Even today, the Dalai Lama successfully threatens to resign as head of the Tibetan people if even one of his fellow citizens harms anyone—it could be to draw attention to their fate as displaced persons. Where else but in Tibet can people claim that they have so much respect for their leader that no plane has been hijacked, no hotel blown up and no politician kidnapped for years to draw attention to the cruel fate of the Tibetans? I will try to make a small contribution to the survival of this wonderful culture with my stories.

Farewell, abandoned, old, lonely city in the snowy mountains—city of a forgotten, mysterious culture, city of believers, Buddhists, Tibetans and great lamas. I feel deep in my heart that you were once my city too, the home of my most beautiful reincarnation.

1

Icons of Peace: A Chance Meeting

I sat firmly strapped into the old, rattling propeller plane of India's Kingfisher Airline.

The airport fireman had taken the precaution of monitoring the take-off of the two propellers with a huge fire extinguisher, while another plane, which had just landed from a place, nearby Amritsar, was taking up its parking position.

As we slowly made our way up to the rather short runway at Kangra Airport, I tried to clean the small, dirty peephole of the roaring aircraft with my handkerchief to catch a moment of this special event.

For the first time, I wish I had missed this flight from this small Himalayan airport to Delhi. I could have been a witness to a historic meeting.

As soon as I checked in, I noticed the huge police presence on the tarmac. I was used to the presence of military jeeps there, but this time something special was going on. Before I could even enquire about what must have been a high-profile visitor, the little stewardess whispered to me: 'Desmond Tutu, the African bishop, is visiting His Holiness the Dalai Lama. Sorry for any complications, sir.' While I thought about what she had just said, she took my ticket and passport and escorted me to the jetway of the plane, which was ready to take off.

I was almost witness to a historic meeting, and only through the dirty windows could I see a group of Buddhist monks walking from the VIP rooms of the airport to the plane that had just landed. I could still see the confusion of dark-skinned, brightly dressed people and the monks from the aircraft that had just taken off. Yes, I was witnessing a special meeting, if only in passing.

After the South African government banned the Dalai Lama from entering the country to visit his friend, the Nobel Peace Prize winner came to visit His Holiness in the Himalayas.

These special moments have taught me over the past twenty-five years, spent with my Buddhist friends in the Himalayas, that it is not material wealth that makes us happy. It is the encounters with people that ascertain our feelings of joy, peace and happiness.

As if in a Bollywood film, the foothills of the Himalayas passed by the peephole in the small plane. Far away on the horizon, I could see the snow-capped peaks, and behind them the land of my Tibetan friends, from which they had been exiled.

I think of Desmond Tutu and the Dalai Lama embracing, always cheerful, always laughing and happy despite their painful past. What wonderful examples of a mostly sad and decaying culture to which I am returning.

It's my Western world that I keep running away from in search of something that doesn't seem to exist there; something I can hold on to and orientate myself by;

something that gives me stability on my emotional roller coaster between the daily struggle to survive through meagre profits, excessive taxes and mostly overburdening bureaucracy to maintain a strange prosperity for people that for me is more like the motorway to decay. The medicine of our time has never been so advanced and successful, there is a cure for every disease. But every disease?

The army of psychologists seems tiny to anyone who has recognised the state of immunity of our mental world. Feelings are dulled, and the world of emotions is lost. What is left is fear, stress and depression. Love, charity and compassion lose their meaning.

Since my countless visits to my Tibetan friends over the last twenty-five years, I have changed from someone who helps to someone who is very happy to receive gifts.

The manuscript of a book I have been writing for more than a quarter of a century is still in my luggage. I would like to share some of my experiences in my search for happiness. 'Learn from monks who have studied the science of the mind for thousands of years. Carry it like a seed into your world,' my friend Rigo Tulku Rinpoche, at Nyingmapa temple in Tso Pema, told me long ago. 'And,' he added, 'do it again and again as long as you live.'

We are already selfish when it comes to bringing up our children. Instead of teaching them to care for others, we set an example of strong selfishness ourselves. We often teach them about 'me, me, me, and then my children' much more than necessary inner values! Just as we try to protect ourselves from physical illness by strengthening our immune system, it is equally necessary to strengthen our mental immunity against negative influences. Love, laughter and happiness are the best defences! This takes a lifetime of training.

I have probably learnt the most about managing my positive and negative emotions during my visits to the villages for Tibetan refugee children. Despite the painful separation from their families, which is often incomprehensible to us, they convey an unparalleled happiness that makes you forget any negative thoughts.

'Switch on your drone,' a wise monk told me, 'and watch how you appear. Then learn to discard negativity.'

The four major human emotions are fear, anger, sadness and joy. The fact that three of them tend to be negative makes the path to happiness all the more difficult.

Our noisy, stressful environment and the negative influence of media of all kinds promote fear, anger and sadness but rarely joy and happiness!

Observe people in our shopping streets and you will rarely see happy faces, even though they are usually carrying bulging shopping bags.

The emotional substages of anxiety, such as depression, have become a widespread disease. The refuge of disguised charity for dogs and cats is usually of little help.

My Tibetan protégés radiate that all-important 'spiritual immunity' and I even find it contagious. The reason behind my travels becomes more apparent coming across these countless positive feelings.

This is one of the biggest reasons I chose to write about my experience—spanning across twenty-five years—with these wonderful people in this book. Perhaps it will help you too in your search for happiness.

2

Preparing for the Journey

The days leading up to a trip to the Tibetan orphanages in the Himalayas of northern India are always some of the most stressful and chaotic of the entire working year. There are many, almost impossible, things that need to be done in order to escape the madness of European rules and regulations for a few weeks.

First, I have to sift through my restaurant's ever-changing reservation lists to see, for example, if I can be excused from important events. It's not uncommon for an important last-minute reservation at work to upset my travel plans. But I'm a quick learner—I already block off the necessary holiday periods in my diary a year before my adventure trip. But even that can go wrong.

New entry visa, no plane ticket without cancellation insurance, constantly repacking my suitcase, constantly checking the weather forecast; daily checks on the political situation in the border region with Pakistan, and India's endless border disputes with its arch-enemy China—looking into all of these become part of the recurring preparations. This is also followed by countless emails with my Tibetan and Indian friends in the Himalayas, including even some Muslim friends besides the usual Hindus and Buddhists. After more than thirty years of adventures in Asia, one learns to travel with an ever-changing checklist.

Despite all these mostly predictable events in my travel destinations, the most unpredictable and annoying ones are those in my beloved homeland of Austria. I am a down-to-earth host but very cosmopolitan. My restaurant in the capital of Upper Austria employs about fifty-six people. They come from seventeen different countries and at least seven different religions. I have the rare pleasure of learning from my foreign employees every day. I want to understand their language and get to know the peculiarities of their culture. Sometimes I get important insider tips, for example, on regional cultural festivals. These also include tips from experienced local guides, whose help I have always appreciated.

Friendly families of my colleagues also invite me for dinner, and I am often allowed to stay with their relatives. There, hospitality is highly valued. I was usually treated like a king, so it wasn't always enjoyable for me. I now realise that they are grateful to me because they know I have helped their children in western Europe in getting a residence permit, an apartment and a job. I have become one of them—a friend and a brother. They know that I am part of a society that allows them to enjoy a little of our seemingly never-ending Western prosperity in the distant Himalayas. In many cases, entire villages live off the wages earned in my inn and sent home by my staff.

I often find myself comparing the friendly and welcoming faces of the people in the Himalayan mountains with those who live in our mostly hermetically sealed apartment blocks back home. These are people who can afford to hide behind concrete walls in their magnificent villas.

No, it's not just about the visits to the Dalai Lama or the invitation from my long-time friend Rigo Tulku Rinpoche Lama* to his beautiful monastery in the Indian Himalayas. It is also about the time to reflect, not to be disturbed by anyone, and to be surrounded by loving people from many different cultures. It is the hours and days spent with the happy children in the huge SOS children's villages set up in Dharamshala. There is an important saying of the Dalai Lama: 'Happiness does not come to those who have much, but to those who have little.' This always makes me wonder whether what I am doing amidst the madness in Europe is right.

I compare the almost shy-looking people in our neighbourhood with the bright smile of a Tibetan schoolchild in the mountains of the northern Himalayas. I wonder about the beautifully landscaped parks and playgrounds that have been built using a significant portion of taxpayers' money for the benefit of our city's children, mothers, families and the elderly. But often they are occupied by loitering alcoholics, youth gangs or drug junkies. This creates fear and drives away those for whom these parks and playgrounds were intended.

The Dalai Lama once jokingly said to me, 'The people in the mountains are honest, friendly and peace-loving. You Austrians are also mountain people like us Tibetans ... even if the mountains are not quite as high for you.' And once again he smiled from the depths of his soul.

Well, he certainly didn't have an opportunity to stroll through our parks and backstreets at night, unlike me who

---

* The asterisks denote terms explained in the Glossary.

carries around a pepper spray for my safety when I go out for a walk. If he were ever to do so, he would realise how unsafe even Europe has become.

We have forgotten how to separate the wheat from the chaff in all the fuss about social welfare. We have forgotten how to distinguish between honest refugees seeking protection and criminal parasites. Not every entrepreneur is the ruthless boss of an exclusively profit-driven, powerful corporation. Many entrepreneurs have been trying for generations to pass on their small and medium-sized businesses to the next generation. Until then, they face a daily struggle for economic survival with their long-serving, loyal employees. In many cases, they need the help of foreign workers. And yes, it is always these moments, thoughts and comparisons that make me reflect on my many trips to the Himalayas. I have decided to capture these moments in writing so that others can share my reflections.

Once again, I couldn't bring the weight of my bags and suitcases under the 30-kg limit set by the airline. Of course, I was carrying a few gifts and souvenirs for my Tibetan refugee children. But I knew very well that eight T-shirts, four pairs of trousers, an anorak, a jacket and a jogging suit for the night, my huge photographic equipment, a toiletry bag and so on were far more than necessary luggage for any Tibetan fleeing across the border. But I come from the West—capitalist, hard-working and strictly brought up by my parents as per the principles of German perfection. Okay, I'm Austrian, so they should be a bit more relaxed. Still, any Tibetan mountain nomad would laugh his head off if he saw what I had packed as 'absolutely necessary'.

Necessary vaccinations are stocked up. I can't imagine being bitten by a dog or scratched by a monkey. Both could transmit rabies. What would happen if you didn't get this life-saving injection within twenty-four hours in one of the hospitals, most of which are far away in the valley? Quite simply, you would die, or rather die miserably. I remember a German woman on a Himalayan trek who died of a simple ruptured appendix due to lack of sanitation. That's exactly why I had it removed as a precaution when I was in hospital years ago. How ridiculous the fears of the countless Covid-19 opponents seem to me.

My friend Martin downloaded a data package from our mobile phone provider. I didn't want to fall into the Indian mobile phone cost trap again. Internet sticks are acquired as well as an iPhone, an Indian phone, a laptop, an iPad, a power station, a camera and lenses, along with many cables and plugs for Indian systems. I also did not forget my two cans of pepper spray. I always carry them with me as a defence against the many annoying street dogs in the small Indian villages. If necessary, I could also use them to scare off any robbers. However, these modest weapons of defence are almost always left behind as a small gift to female hitchhikers in India.

Soon, the visa for India was arranged, and travel and repatriation insurance were obtained. As so often, I discussed inheritance matters and a necessary will with my lawyer—you never know! I stay up to date with the telephone numbers of the Austrian Embassy and the Austrian Trade Delegation in Delhi. All my Indian and Tibetan friends were informed in advance about my visit.

I have a whole series of other 'vital' phone contacts on my Austrian mobile phone: doctors, first-aid specialists, my bank manager, journalists and well-known former ambassadors and trade delegates. Every Indian guest who has visited my restaurant is skilfully lured so that addresses can eventually be exchanged. Networking is my speciality. It is the foundation of my professional success and the basis of my many friends in the Himalayas. Over the years, my checklist for travelling to India has become very long. But I have also learnt to leave unnecessary baggage at home. Prudence, discipline and common sense are usually more useful than some life-saving equipment. And then there are my countless friends who would move mountains to help me in my time of need.

Nevertheless, I made arrangements for my wife Monika to receive a text message every day around the same time, just to confirm that I am doing fine—sometimes, this dependant on the network.

Soon, I was on the train to the airport. Still a little relaxed, I went through all the preparations again in my head. Not forgetting anything is incredibly important in such a situation—check, check, check … like a pilot before take-off. Everything was perfect. A tender feeling of happiness overcame me. The journey ahead was to take me to my dream destination.

3

Dangerous Indian Roads

Unfortunately, the few flights from Delhi to Dharamshala were again cancelled due to bad weather. Thankfully, I had wisely asked my long-time friend Mohit to send us a jeep. The driver was patiently waiting outside Delhi airport at two o'clock in the morning. He was to take us to the Kullu Valley, some 400 km away. It would have normally taken ten long hours to drive that distance. Luckily, we didn't realise at the time that it would take almost fifteen hours this time due to the bad roads and the onset of monsoon rains. After all, it had been sixteen hours since we had left Linz. The journey to the airport in Vienna, the check-in at the airport, the flight to Delhi and now travelling by jeep on bad roads—it was going to be a very long day! I was used to such journeys by now. However, it was different for my fellow travellers, resulting in me getting a real headache. I could only hope that they would hold out.

The temperature in Delhi was 36°C, even though it was night time! It was even hotter during the day, going up to 46 °C the day before. I knew why I had chosen to travel at night. But even that was proving to be difficult. Six hours more, and we would reach Chandigarh, the capital of Punjab and Haryana.

The nights were humid, with heavy downpours time and again. It is likely that the monsoon arrived sooner than anticipated. Good for agriculture, bad for us. Before the monsoon, the whole country was dry as dust and parched. The rain turned the roads into a slippery surface. It was a difficult journey for our chauffeur as we drove on roads that were flooded and hard to see. Our driver was swearing to himself the whole time. Despite the night journey, there was an incredible amount of lorry traffic. Sometimes there were endless traffic jams because of terrible accidents. Sensible drivers avoid these dangerous night-time journeys altogether. It is easier to travel during the day. But we were on a tight schedule—which didn't make things any easier. I was on my way to the Tibetan children's villages near Dharamshala with a small film crew. The crew wanted to make a documentary about my Tibetan orphanage projects. This was, I believe, my seventeenth visit to this amazing nation in seventeen years.

We came across a site of an accident! A smaller, fully loaded lorry had struck a larger lorry in front of it. Probably a result of exhaustion. The cab of the smaller lorry looked terrible—totally smashed. The driver, who must have been badly injured, was lying on blankets on the damp road in the dim light, with nothing to protect him. Hundreds of cars whizzed past him at far too high a speed. Any consideration for him and the rescuers on the road, which was only dimly lit by headlights? Not a chance!

Once again I realised how difficult it is to get help here. On the other hand, how great are our social facilities, such as the ambulance service, the emergency helicopter, the police and the fire brigade, which are frequently required. Even if all this costs a lot of taxpayers' money and requires the commitment of volunteers, you quickly get the support you need. Unfortunately, things were different here. Lucky are those who realise in time that their health depends mainly on their own caution.

About thirty minutes later, many kilometres further on, we spotted a small, old vehicle on the modest motorway. It was an ambulance, making its way along the makeshift roadside, at high speed and with its blue lights flashing dimly. Help was in sight. But where was the nearest hospital? We were doubtful that there was a doctor in the car.

I often think about how alone and helpless you can get, especially if you fall ill or have an accident. It's best not to think about it at all ... and yes, caution is the only thing that can be of help in such circumstances.

We hoped to reach our destination safely and without any further problems. The thought that our driver had already travelled eight hours from faraway Shimla and would be behind the wheel for another four hours made me worry. So I decided to keep an eye on him rather than the surroundings. Unfortunately, he didn't speak a word of English. Conversely, we had the same problem with Hindi. So we tried to converse through gestures and body language, something that foreign travellers have successfully practised for thousands of years. It's good enough for small talk but certainly not for addressing real problems. I was still carrying in my mobile phone the contact numbers of many friends in the Himalayas. I desperately wished I didn't have to use any of those.

All the roads to Chandigarh were now almost impassable due to the extremely heavy rain and countless torrents. Even the jeep could only move at a walking pace. Eventually we climbed into the first foothills of the Himalayas, and morning slowly crept up on us. We drove through small Indian villages and children waved at us as they went to school. Everything suddenly seemed so much more peaceful. The hectic traffic, the eerie darkness of the night had all left their mark. But during the short breaks we took to drink chai, we began to forget all of the unpleasantness.

I already knew one of my travelling companions from a local TV station in Linz. Anna, a young film-maker, she had already made successful travel documentaries about Costa Rica and the slums of South Africa. Luckily, she was an experienced traveller. Her cameraman, however, was younger than her and probably on his first trip of this kind. Anna was quite serious about the idea of making a film about the children of Tibet and their fate. I liked that. Such an endeavour in the depths of the Himalayas would be possible only by approaching it with personal commitment. So I decided to finance the flights and their stay out of my own pocket. I was sure that backing a film about the life of children in the northern Himalayas would benefit the Tibetan people more than funding solar panels or similar projects for a few thousand euros. The world cannot learn enough about how hard it is for these people to preserve their unique culture.

I have often met top bosses in Tibet. After a successful business life, many of them had only one goal in mind: to learn about the Tibetan monks' Buddhist philosophy of life and their culture dating back to thousands of years, in order to try to apply those teachings in their own lives. After years of costly seminars and expensive management training, many have come here to learn the true values of life.

Contentment, tolerance and charity are treasures that this culture has cultivated, taught and passed on from one generation to the next. Perhaps I could use the film to help people back home understand why Tibetan mothers in Chinese-occupied Tibet often send their only children on the long journey over the endless snow-capped mountains to the Dalai Lama. What is more important than true maternal love? Is it the knowledge of 'human spiritual life' that has been practised and passed down since time immemorial, and the learning and passing on of these peaceful experiences that have been gathered here in the Himalayas for centuries?

For us westerners, this is often incomprehensible. But we have the Tibetan people to thank for the fact that we can, if we wish, make use of these precious legacies in our sadly hectic and stressed-out world.

Before nightfall, we reached the legendary Naggar Castle, perched high above the valley. Of course, we could have stayed in the old guest house of the Tibetan Thangka Painting School in Patlikuhal. Unfortunately, it was a bit run-down. But after the hardships of the journey, I wanted to offer my fellow travellers a more comfortable place to stay, at least for the first night.

4

At the Tibetan Thangka Painting School

We left early in the morning. Together with Angela, an Austrian film director, I wanted to visit the nearby Tibetan Thangka Painting School in the small Indian village of Patlikul.

No, it's not a beautiful school building. In fact, the huge square building with a makeshift courtyard on the northern slope of the Himalayas in the Kullu Valley resembles a post-war military barracks.

This school is trying to keep alive the ancient art of Tibetan scroll painting, even with limited resources. Thangkas are painstakingly painted with semi-precious stones using a centuries-old tradition.

The modest income from sales is nowhere near enough to fund the lengthy training programme. Without outside support, it will soon be impossible to continue this ancient art.

My long-time friend Norgyal Choephel was already waiting for us at the entrance to the school. We embraced happily; Norgyal took my hand in the loving Tibetan way and we strolled back to the school gate holding hands like a couple in love, the jeep following us. He doesn't let go of my hand the entire way. We hadn't seen each other for almost a year, so we had a lot to talk about.

Almost seventy, Norgyal was the head of the Tibetan school, and was to retire soon. As a child, he too had made the long journey from Lhasa with the fleeing Dalai Lama.

His life has been eventful. He took every opportunity to tell me about his arduous journey in the early 1960s. He knew that I wished to write a book about my travels to meet my Tibetan friends. I instantly knew that he was thinking about something similar. Norgyal smiled at me and said, 'Yes, just like His Holiness's teacher, Mr Heinrich Harrer, in *Seven Years in Tibet*,' while nodding his head and holding my hand.

I knew how important it was for Norgyal to feed me with as much information as possible so that, through my planned book, the world could understand the suffering that economic greed and political obsession with power had inflicted on his people. Yes, it was my aim to pen down such stories of my many Tibetan friends.

Few people are aware of the deliberate destruction of this culture of an ancient doctrine of spiritual science and Buddhist philosophy of life. How childish and superficial the standardised bookish knowledge of our latitudes often seems.

But there is at least a small spark of hope, which I have been able to experience through the traditions of Tibetan eyewitnesses, whom I have met again and again during my almost twenty-five years of visits in the Himalayas. I would like to do my bit, like Heinrich Harrer, the Jesuit priest Johann

Grueber from Linz, and many other travellers who also felt the need to pass down what they experienced, to give others the chance to learn from what was handed down.

The Buddhism practised in Tibet today was introduced by Padmasambhava, a Buddhist monk and reincarnate, in the eighth century. He taught the Tibetans to abandon the worship of spirits and idols, to focus on the new teachings of reformed Buddhism and, of course, to pass on and transmit this knowledge from father to son, from mother to daughter and from daughter to her children.

A vast treasure of knowledge, insight and wisdom unimaginable to mankind, a legacy for man and nature accumulated over the centuries, protected by insurmountable borders of ice and snow, mostly impregnable mountain massifs, endless mountain deserts and impenetrable primeval forests, this special knowledge had been passed on and guarded since time immemorial.

This awareness was reinforced by the difficulty of even entering the place. For generations, visiting this territory without permission was punishable by death. Since then, very few non-Tibetans have managed to bring knowledge or accounts of the life of these mysterious mountain people to our latitudes.

Through my many visits to the Himalayas, I too have become one of the privileged few who have been able to learn about the legacy of history directly from those who were affected and survived.

What is it that makes the Chinese, probably one of the largest and most powerful nations in the world, so afraid of the revered God-King, the Dalai Lama, and of the mysterious Tibetan culture and the small number of Tibetan people compared to them? Are they afraid of a loving, peaceful and an always smiling monk like the Dalai Lama, a living god without military hardware like missiles and tanks but only equipped with an arsenal of love, compassion and tolerance?

How easy it would be to defeat huge armies and their generals if more people made these invincible 'weapons' or, like my Tibetan friends, helped to preserve, exchange and learn from this wonderful heritage.

As I met Norgyal Choephel again, I felt my conscience speak to me once more: *Do something, write about it; the stories of Heinrich Harrer are history, stories of a time long gone, and yet more relevant and real than ever.* I felt the need to tell people that absolutely nothing has changed since the Dalai Lama fled his homeland of Tibet in 1959 more than 60 years ago, that humanity has learned absolutely nothing, and tell them that many of today's refugees want to do the opposite of those who fled Tibet! Many wished to take their religion to another culture, many wanted to sow their political interests, conquer new lands, and nibble and profit from the hard-earned wealth of a hard-working generation.

No political and religious leader of our so-called progressive Western capitalist world can claim that his followers practise and follow principles similar to those of the Tibetans.

***

The Thangka Painting School in Patlikul currently has around sixty Tibetan boys and girls, and the number is growing. A tightly knit artistic programme ensures that young Tibetan artists receive a good education. There is also a small sewing school for girls.

While conducting interviews for her film on Tibet, my companion talked to some curious Tibetan boys who had managed to escape from Tibet. Most of them talked about wanting to return home after their education. Of course, this is rarely possible, as the penalties for those seeking to return are too high and the few passports that can be obtained are too strictly controlled. However, they continue dreaming of returning to their homeland and their families.

With my modest aid project and the support of many friends, I had financed solar panels, so that the children could have at least a lukewarm shower, especially during the freezing winter months. We had even bought computer equipment, so that they could keep in touch with the happenings in Dharamshala or their relatives around the world. However, during one of my visits a year later, the boxed personal computers (PCs) were still found under the office desk—there was no money for a specialist to network and assemble them.

Of course, I took care of that too, and soon a computer specialist from the next town arrived and installed everything. Today, I really enjoy corresponding with the children via emails in my broken English.

I am particularly proud of the many touching drawings of their escape that they have continued to send me. I hope that one day they will adorn the cover of one of my books. It's moving how the children have captured their terrible escape in pictures. The pictures repeatedly depict enormous, limitless mountains and impressively large herds of yaks. You can see the children marching in long rows, one behind the other, across vast snowfields towards their long-awaited freedom.

In almost each of these drawings, shockingly accurate and recognisable Chinese soldiers with rifles lurk behind rocks, and there are always large pools of red blood and very realistically painted dead children.

In a frighteningly accurate, yet almost childlike innocence, the Tibetan children seem to be coming to terms with what they have experienced, which they will probably never forget.

I also recall many Austrians and Tibetans protesting against the fact that these Chinese military units were receiving special training alongside Austrian mountain troops in the Carinthian Alps at the time!

Unfortunately, we Austrians and Europeans have often forgotten what happened to our mothers and fathers not so long ago when, after the fall of the Nazi regime, foreign military forces prevented them from visiting family members in other occupied zones.

Thanks to committed and fearless politicians and people with charisma and backbone, we still have our mother tongue and can continue to practise our culture. They were great personalities who fought for our freedom, but today we search in vain for such role models.

During one of his last visits to Austria, our then head of state repeatedly refused to receive the Nobel Peace Prize winner, the Dalai Lama, with embarrassing and flimsy excuses. This very leader should know better about our country's sad past.

Where are the world's great statesmen? Is it more important to support the greed of corrupt financial jugglers, banks, states and military powers than to uphold the much-vaunted human rights? All these thoughts ran through my mind as I travelled to the exiled homeland of my Tibetan friends.

Norgyal, the headmaster, showed me around the classrooms. I saw young artists sitting on the floor on thick blankets, with thangka paintings in wooden frames in front of them. They were busy creating artworks in accordance with strict traditional Buddhist guidelines.

Next to them were several little jars and glass bowls of rich, uncommon hues, produced from semi-precious stones such as malachite and turquoise, found and processed in the vast mountain communities of Ladakh that, according to Norgyal, always follow the same protocol.

To make a thangka, the students need a precise knowledge of the centuries-old iconographic rules of measurements and proportions of Buddhist figures. The diversity of Tibetan Buddhism encompasses thousands of different figures. No artist, however experienced, can know all the characteristics of every deity. A coordinate grid is therefore often used as an aid to make free sketching of the main figures.

Hundreds of shades of a single colour are then applied to stretched canvases with wafer-thin brushes across months of painstaking work.

To fulfil its function as a sacred object, the finished painting is framed in a textile frame, often made of Chinese silk, and then hung on a leather strap. These are made by Tibetan refugee girls in an adjacent tailoring workshop. A thin veil, sewn only at the top, protects the thangka against the dust and smoke from the butter lamps in the dark monasteries. This veil is then rolled up like a curtain during ceremonies.

According to devout Buddhists, a consecration breathes life into the work of art! The image on the thangka is charged with spiritual energy, and the depicted deity's eyes are opened to receive all sentient beings.

Buyers from large galleries in the main centres of India and Nepal select the best pieces and sell them to collectors for a lot of money. Every time I visit, I buy some of this art, as it is often the only source of income for the Tibetans living here.

The situation is not very different for carpet weavers in Kashmir and many ancient cultures around the world. Young people tend to see better opportunities as IT specialists and naturally wish to opt for that. Thus, the ancient Tibetan art of thangka painting is dying out. Not many people are practising this uncommon craft into old age, and it will soon be forgotten in our fast-paced world—what a pity, another culture is disappearing.

For our farewell, we were treated to a dance performance in the old school hall. Dressed in the sumptuous national costume of the ancient Tibetans, about twenty young people proudly performed Tibetan folk dances for us, accompanied by an ancient, croaking music system.

The high-pitched and almost melancholic singing of the group of Tibetan girls always gives me goosebumps. These songs passed down from the parents to their children seem to be filled with so much sadness. They sing of snow-capped peaks, of huge herds of yaks and of working the barren grain fields. The work in the fields is incorporated into their dance movements.

They sing of long, freezing nights spent with their families in winter camps, and their songs tell of the miracles of famous lamas or spiritual healers. They have lost their homeland, but they have carried the songs of their families with them to pass down to their children, as they have been doing for generations. China has robbed them of their homeland, but the seeds of their culture will now be scattered around the world.

I found it hard to hide my tears. I couldn't—why should I have? My friend Norgyal noticed my teary face; he smiled and took my hands lovingly in his, as he often did. Why do these Tibetan songs touch me so much. Is it the memory of a past time, of a previous life? I am sure that if Buddhist reincarnation and the doctrine of rebirths really exist, then yes, I was perhaps one of them.

Thank you, Tibet!

5

At the Corpse Pass

I had visited the historic Kullu Valley* in the 1990s. At that time, the valley would be mainly lit by stinking, smoking gas and oil lamps, which provided only dim light for the simple dwellings of the inhabitants. Electric lighting was almost non-existent. Today, however, huge changes are afoot. Huge dams are being built. Attempts are being made to tame the raging mountain river Beas, which rises at the top of the 4,000-m Rohtang Pass*, and to generate much-needed electricity.

The country has a huge appetite for energy, and it needs to be fed. The journey through this otherwise romantic and mysterious valley is marred by dirty-looking settlements resulting from countless construction sites.

Near the Rohtang Pass, the warriors of Alexander the Great are said to have refused to follow their general after a fierce battle. After all, he wanted to extend his empire to the ends of the earth, which, according to the ideas of the time, lay beyond this mighty Himalayan massif. The intimidating snow-capped peaks and the few crossings into distant Ladakh were probably the winners of this legendary campaign initiated by one of the greatest generals of all time.

Whether the reason for his return was anger at the refusal of his comrades-in-arms or deep grief at the loss of his beloved warhorse, Bucephalus, is unknown. Even the historical legends laconically report that 'Alexander did not leave his tent for several days' and eventually 'decided to withdraw his weakened army'.

History is silent as to whether Roxane was the real reason for Alexander's long stay in the warmth of the field tent. It is said that Alexander married the beautiful Himalayan girl much against the wishes of his Macedonian friends—after all, Roxane was the daughter of his enemy. Her father, the Bactrian chieftain Oxyartes, had taken her to safety from Alexander's army in the rock castle of Ariamazes, which was thought to be impregnable. However, Alexander took over the castle and then captured Roxane. This had consequences for the beautiful princess. The most sought-after bachelor of his time is said to have fallen in love with her at first sight. Roxane must have had a similar experience: she remained loyal to Alexander until his death, accompanying him on his campaigns.

In retrospect, it was probably the best decision Alexander could have made. Even today, the dreaded Rohtang Pass is only passable for a few months of the year.

For thousands of years, caravans have travelled from the ancient Chinese imperial city of Xi'an in the direction from which Alexander's army once came. The route is part of the legendary Silk Road and an important trade route to European countries, at the start of which lies the town of Manali*. 'Manali Road' is still used today as a derogatory term for the bad roads in the Himalayas. I came to understand the reason behind this—deep potholes and huge boulders lying around often make it impossible to get through. Hundreds of migrant workers from the eastern India are constantly repairing and mending the roads.

On my first visit, I saw that huge boulders blocking the road were still being painstakingly split and crushed by hand with hammers and chisels. The women and children of the migrant workers, hailing from distant Bihar, would then process the crushed rock until it could finally be used as a base for tarred roads. That was the only way to prevent it from being washed away during the next monsoon. Today, this heavy work is done by powerful Caterpillar machines. This is mainly in the interest of the Indian military. The few connecting roads to the endless borders with neighbouring China have to be guarded and protected. Countless columns of military trucks transport soldiers, ammunition and rations to the border area. Insiders say there are around a million Indian and Chinese soldiers stationed up there.

I tried taking a day's rest before the arduous and dangerous crossing of the Rohtang Pass. Manali is on the verge of becoming a unique winter resort in the Himalayas, thanks to its long-lasting snow cover. There are even some old ski lifts. What comes as a complete surprise, however, is that you can hire second-hand skis, all of which are brought from Austria and are perfect for putting your skiing skills to test on the rather unkempt slopes. Together with the head of the Austrian Ski Team, Hans Pum, I too helped deliver a container of partly used skis and equipment. Today, these skis are used by the Indian and Tibetan residents of the village. Interestingly, Aanchal Thakur, also an inhabitant, showed off her skills at the Winter Olympics. She trained in Austria for the Olympic Games in China. We may have helped her a little.

***

Ugly Indian guest houses with fancy-sounding names, such as Hilton, Paradiso and Snow Leopard, await guests from the country's hot and noisy big cities. But what fun we had when my friend Leo and I stayed in one of these dreadful places on one of my first visits.

While the whole town watched the cricket final between arch-enemies India and Pakistan on the old black-and-white television sets, I tried to fix the broken ceiling lamp in my room. Had I known that my amateurish repair skills would have knocked out the power supply to the whole house, I might have gone to bed with my torch. Thankfully, no one realised who was responsible. The fanatical Indian sports fans would have lynched us.

Kullu Valley is also one of India's last great drug paradises. Hemp grows by the roadside like stinging nettles. It is believed that there are huge, well-hidden opium fields in the deep valleys. It appears as if the last of the hippies have moved up from far-off Goa. Tattered posters with photos of missing hitchhikers hang from the old, shabby wooden huts—but nobody cares because most of them have settled in the wide valleys of the Himalayas. No one wants to be 'found' there.

Come evenings, the dimly lit atmosphere reminded me of a horror film. Shepherds would spend the night with their flocks in the market square, guarded by huge Himalayan dogs. Long, shaggy figures in wide coats scurried through the narrow streets. Bearded men watched me while I tried not to look anyone in the eyes for the simple reason that I didn't want to provoke a fight. These were proud men from different cultures. And I was a stranger, and that too a white one. I could sense that I was not welcome. On closer inspection, I noticed that almost everyone was carrying a knife. My ridiculous can of pepper spray, which I had brought with me to deal with the aggressive dogs, was of little use now.

I felt transported to a land from a time long ago. Not much could have changed in this culture in the last few millennia. The fact that I still had the opportunity to immerse myself and be a part of what the nomads and caravans experienced touched me deeply. I became part of a journey through time that is coming to an abrupt end because of progress. I can still see them, the dark figures illuminated by torches and campfires. I can smell the scent of spices from all over the world. I can hear the cries of children and the murmur of sheep and goat herders. I could hear the stories of the past. Soon the pack mules and horses would be replaced by cars. Thousands of tourists from the big cities would storm the paradise in the Himalayas. A world that I could still feel and sense would be lost and forgotten.

I am grateful for getting to experience it all.

Manali and Kullu are the last two major towns before the dreaded Rohtang Pass, which is almost 4,000-metre high and leads through the Pir Panjal mountains into the interior of the western Himalayas. Depending on weather conditions, the pass is closed during the months of October to June. It usually takes four to six weeks to reopen this vital passage. During this time, workers employed in the summer as road construction crews try to clear the incredible masses of snow from the passage.

For years, attempts have been made to cut a giant tunnel through this huge mountain. Again, this is more of a military necessity, but in this case it will benefit all the inhabitants of the region. It was such a pleasure to see the signs of an Austrian construction company which was bringing in its expertise and experience in tunnelling. However, the constant movement of the youngest mountain massif in the Himalayas has repeatedly delayed the ambitious project for years.

The Rohtang Pass is popularly known as the 'corpse pass'. It was given its chilling name in the previous century when a British garrison of about a hundred soldiers died here in one of the dreaded blizzards. Today, some twenty-five years after my first visit, much has changed. In the summer months, rich Indians from distant Delhi and Mumbai flee the intense heat to the few remaining glacial remnants in the mountain villages around the Kullu Valley.

Many Tibetans make a living as tourist guides. For tourists in the freezing weather, they make for great photo opportunities with their shaggy yaks. This also helps them earn a few extra rupees. For the three to four-hour trip up the Rohtang Pass, you can rent thick, well-worn coats—usually infested with bugs and lice—from small shops. None of the Indian tourists come with the necessary warm clothing.

Such an excursion can often end badly. Entire stretches of road disappear under huge mudslides, and jeeps, lorries or minibuses get swept away. I've also had to cancel my travel plans several times. Up there, I met the puny, dark-skinned migrants from the distant, very poor Indian state of Bihar. During the short summer months, they would come up here with their entire families to work on road construction for a meagre wage.

Even from a distance you can see the huge clouds of smoke arising from the stinking, poisonous, boiling asphalt molasses being prepared in tin cans, in which the crushed rock fragments are stirred and later poured on to the road to repair it, in a haphazard way. The Bihari workers are unaware of the risk to their lungs. All they care about is the meagre pay they receive from the military for maintaining the vital link to the Himalayas. For many of these families who have travelled a long distance, it is often the only way to earn some money.

These people cannot survive for long. No lung can withstand breathing in the toxic tar mixture for long. How ridiculous that the Indian government has just posted a no-smoking sign on the simple tents that are in fact set up only for short durations.

In the style of a suspenseful Hitchcock horror film, long-necked vultures and giant eagles perch on the branches of the bare trees by the side of the Rohtang road as if waiting for their prey. The shepherds know why they carry a rifle. Mountain leopards and Himalayan bears are the biggest enemies of the huge herds of sheep and goats in this sparsely populated region. In the northern Indian state of Himachal Pradesh, many of the rare predators are allegedly shot by poachers and sold on to rich Chinese. The bones and entrails are then processed into exclusive sexual enhancers and sold at exorbitant prices.

I once overheard a conversation between former high-ranking local politicians. They told me that under Indira Gandhi's political leadership, it was ordered that 'if a single one of these rare animals was shot, it would cost the job of the local politician responsible'. Now, new governments are in power and none of these corrupt politicians are missing out on such additional sources of income.

Shepherds on the road to the Rohtang Pass earn extra money by selling precious Himalayan saffron and marmot tallow at the few resting places. Rare minerals can be found by the roadside. Monoliths littered with beautiful fossilised sea creatures are evidence that there was once a vast ocean on the site of the world's highest mountain range.

I remember the many stories about the Tibetan mountain antelope (*chiru*), which is almost extinct now. Today, the few surviving specimens are strictly protected. Money-hungry poachers have simply shot them to extinction in the barren mountain deserts of the vast, unmanageable and lonely valleys.

The woolly hair on the neck of the Tibetan antelope is considered the finest of all animal hairs. It takes the wool from three to five animals to make one shawl (*shahtoosh*). Although trading 'products' of these animals has long been banned, many people in Tibetan and north Indian weaving mills still make a living from the illegal production of such shawls. Incidentally, a raid on a charity event in New York led to the arrest of super-rich people, models and celebrities who had illegally bought such shawls for up to $10,000.

High in the mountains, shepherds face a tough time collecting the precious wool left behind by the animals as they feed on the few thorny bushes. It often takes years to collect enough to weave a valuable scarf. It is only this 'collected' treasure that they can sell in the black market. Today, attempts are being made to reintroduce and breed the rare animals in large, cordoned-off areas.

In order to visit the renowned Kye Monastery and the highest point in India with electricity, I wanted to continue the journey from Manali in the Kullu Valley over the Rohtang Pass. From there, I intended to travel to Kibber, which is roughly 5,500 meters above sea level, to the hospital. We had just driven through beautiful meadows. I was admiring the splendour of the countless flowers, even edelweiss, when thick fog descended from the surrounding peaks into the enchanting valley. My driver kept the pace to a minimum to avoid making any driving mistakes. Such mistakes can quickly prove to be fatal. I looked out of the window, worriedly. The road to the left plunged downhill for hundreds of metres. Apart from that, all you could see was thick, white, sloping fog. Most of the valley crossings had been blasted out of the rock and were so narrow that usually only one jeep could pass. But my driver was watching the sheer cliffs on the upper side. I knew that the far greater danger was the falling rocks that kept blocking our path. We smiled with relief as we neared another valley ahead.

We took a break at one of the roadside *dhabas* (small stone tents) and drank some chai. My driver wanted to enquire about the possibility of continuing our journey. The locals at the dhaba had apparently been around in the area for some time. He soon returned with bad news. The damp air from the valley had caused several mudslides. All the workers had gathered at the top to rescue the three jeeps and their occupants, who were believed to be buried. There was not much hope. Mudslides are caused by loose soil over crumbling rock. Prolonged heavy rainfall, caused by massive climate change, accelerates this process. The soil absorbs the water like a sponge. When it becomes too heavy, it detaches from the rocky ground and thunders down into the valley. In most cases, the masses of earth sweep away the loose rock and the few ancient cedar trees that hold it all together. The mass rolls downhill like a huge, destructive cocktail of soil, debris, rocks and trees. This usually has serious implications and serves as a catalyst for another disaster. The debris flow blocks the mountain rivers, which are normally flooded by melting snow. The water keeps on piling up until the artificial dam bursts like a champagne cork and rushes down the valley as a dreaded rock tsunami. This is often the reason why houses in the area are built well above the water-bearing mountain streams.

I already suspected what Babel, my driver, would tell me, his face wrinkled with sadness: 'Sir, no chance to go to Spiti. Rohtang is closed for weeks, many people dead, too dangerous.'

That was the adventure I sought while travelling in the Himalayas. But it is also the humility I have learnt in over twenty-five years there—nature always wins. That day, the Rohtang Pass didn't allow us to cross it. At the turn of the century, in 1899–1900, a hundred British soldiers on the Rohtang Pass faithfully followed their officer's orders. Their reward was death, and thus the name Corpse Pass. Their bones may have started their journey into the sheltered valley with the mudslide we came to know about on our journey. To be on the safe side, I went back to sit inside the jeep with my friend Babel. I prayed to Buddha and Shiva that we reach the valley safely. I bid my farewell to Rohtang La, promising to come back.

6

First Meeting with the Dalai Lama

I was travelling in Ladakh*, on the border of what was once Tibet, with my friend Leo, an Austrian policeman.

We had a long, arduous journey while crossing the dreaded Rohtang Pass. Via Keylong, we were on our way to Leh, the capital of this valley at an altitude of around 4,000 metres. Our journey took us through the northern Himalayas, dotted with Indian military bases. Leo was in the back of the jeep. We had just crossed Khardung La, one of the highest passes in the world when we found that my companion was suffering from the dreaded altitude sickness.

Suddenly we were stopped by the military post. Roadblock! We were not sure how that happened. So, frustrated, we waited in our cramped jeep for half an hour without being told the reason for the roadblock. Many military personnel, armed with machine guns, were standing right in front of us. Local onlookers had gathered, and we waited for what was to come. My poor English was only good enough to talk about the most essential things, so I sent Babel to talk to the soldiers. I wanted to know the reason for our involuntary halt. Soon he returned with a grin: 'His Holiness the Dalai Lama is coming!'

I almost jumped out of my seat. Had Babel just said the Dalai Lama was coming? Stunned, I first woke up my suffering travelling companion, then we grabbed our cameras and ran straight for the military barrier.

How was this possible? Here at the end of the world, on a rumbling gravel road in the endless Himalayan mountains, right on the border of his homeland occupied by the Chinese military, I was to meet this mysterious God-King! What an incredibly rare stroke of luck.

Then they came—an Indian military escort accompanying the Buddhist religious leader who was so open-hearted and always smiling. The fourteenth reincarnation of the Buddha, the living God-King of the Tibetan people, Nobel Peace Prize winner and the greatest public enemy of the Chinese government.

About six, no, more than eight jeeps were escorting the convoy and turning left in front of our eyes. It was only then that I saw the many snow-white stupas, burial grounds for high-ranking Buddhist dignitaries, standing on a lush green meadow in the nearby valley. They looked to me like alien flying objects, waiting to take off into the vastness of the infinite cosmos. Just behind them was a beautiful Tibetan building. I later found out that it was the house where His Holiness always spends his holidays during the hot summer months.

The Dalai Lama's jeep was easy to spot as he drove past the crowds of Tibetan devotees who had come from afar. With folded hands, he greeted the onlookers waiting by the roadside from the jeep window. He seemed to be smiling at me, and I bowed my head with folded hands following some innate instinct, without taking my eyes off him. My mind wandered as we left the scene of that very special, if sadly brief, encounter in the Himalayas. I closed my eyes and then opened them in disbelief. But, it wasn't a dream—I had met the Dalai Lama.

Information travels fast there even without computers, emails, text messages or telephones. For thousands of years, it has 'flown' over mountains and valleys to the remotest parts of the Himalayas. But to this day, no one knows exactly how this 'system' works.

We came from Shimla, the capital town of Himachal Pradesh, hill station built by the British colonial government. We had spent many days travelling through the territory of the Kinnaur people who belong to a special legendary race. Tall, with almost golden skin and bright blue eyes, these are proud men and beautiful women. They are said to be the descendants of Alexander's warriors. Since time immemorial, they have lived in seclusion in the vast, inaccessible valleys of the Himalayas. For centuries, they have existed as a community of related families within which they also 'reproduce'. They are self-sufficient and avoid contact with the ever-increasing tourism in the region.

As the driver drove towards our destination of Leh, I had a strange, realistic dream. I thought of the many people in our European latitudes who, at the age of forty-five, often take their flight into government-sponsored early retirement. In the prime of their life, full of energy, with valuable knowledge, decades of experience and economic expertise, they enjoy their much too early retirement at the taxpayers' expense. They do nothing, are under-challenged, and eventually suffer from poor health as a result.

Leo, my travelling companion, had told me that he too was retiring early from the police force because of the government's supposedly necessary austerity measures. The state's social regulations allowed him to do this at the age of fifty-nine.

I had worked just as hard for just as long but still had to work off a growing mountain of debt. My son, who is also my designated successor, has three small children. Handing over the reins was still a long way away. Why should I? I enjoyed my work, even if the ever-growing avalanche of bureaucracy sometimes dampened my enthusiasm.

The huge pub with the beer garden stayed open seven days a week. I often had to deal with criticism from customers that we employed 'too many foreigners'. 'Can't you manage to employ more Austrians?' I was often asked patronisingly. Well, with an unemployment rate of just under 5 per cent, it translates to around 450,000 people in our small Austria, which means a really bad fate for many. No work, no job, no money for the family, no future, no vision! But when you read the job advertisements in the local newspapers, you wonder why so many companies are looking for employees in all kinds of professions when several people are registered as unemployed. In my industry, this means that waiters and cooks must work weekends, evenings and nights. That's when other people go out or have time off and want to have fun.

A few years ago, these jobs were hotly contested by enthusiastic and almost always cheerful Austrian staff, but today I can no longer run my business without my foreign staff. Sadly, it took only a few years for some of these colleagues to realise that it was possible to 'nibble' at the huge social cake and live in prosperity without working.

What if police officers, doctors, pilots and people in similarly vital professions were to indulge in such an irresponsible work-life balance? People do not hesitate before giving doctors a call after midnight; or before calling a policeman for pointless arguments, that too without thinking how early or late in the day it is; and booking in family hotels without taking into account the fact that the dates fall on public holidays or church feasts.

Prosperity has made us forget what we did to achieve it. I often think of guests who leave their plates full of delicacies and then go on to grumble about the mountains of discarded yet perfectly recyclable food in the catering and food industry. These are the people who have brought this crime of affluence upon themselves, facilitated by the legal regulations of their politicians.

When I return from one of my trips to the Himalayas, I fondly remember the happy faces of the children who live there. I cannot forget that grateful laughter when I handed over one of my colourful 'Josef balloons' to a little Tibetan refugee girl. Once back in my so-called progressive, civilised homeland, I saw the many unhappy, spoilt children being showered with toys. It was then that I'd again miss that hearty, youthful laughter, the childlike, grateful joy of my Tibetan children. Only those who have travelled there can tell you about it.

Your Holiness, even if I only caught a brief glimpse as I drove by, it was a very special day in my life, and I have you to thank for it.

Back then I didn't know what wonderful encounters with you would follow.

7

Jakob in the Mountains

Far above McLeodganj, high in the Himalayas, an Austrian man has been living with his extremely kind German wife for almost forty years. Jakob came to India as a student in the late hippie era and met his wife. Today, he earns his living by organising trips to the nearby Himalayas or to destinations further afield. These are adventure tours of a special kind. Sometimes he sends me greetings from Timbuktu in the Sahara, sometimes from Ethiopia or the Chinese Silk Road. He rarely travels to Europe.

Jakob has three wonderful sons. They all went to school at the nearby SOS Children's Village and also studied with the many Tibetan refugee kids in McLeodganj. They speak fluent English, Hindi and, of course, perfect Tibetan. Their mother tongue is German. All three boys have chosen wonderful vocations. Then there is the adopted Tibetan daughter who Jakob and Felicitas have welcomed into the family. This 'Austrian–German family' lives on an Indian farm high in the

Himalayas. Long before that, the farm was the summer home of the former US ambassador from Amritsar during the hot summer months back in the days of the British occupation. It lies above the Tibetan SOS Children's Village of McLeodganj, on the summit of a mountain almost 3,000 metres high. Jakob's parents are from Tyrol and Vienna. His grandfather was a well-known surgeon at the Sisters of Mercy Hospital in Linz. It's remarkable how many Austrians you meet all over the world.

If you visit Jakob in May, as I did, you walk through a blooming mountain of red rhododendrons. I've had the pleasure of visiting him many times. My first visit was many years ago. I was travelling with my son Andreas to visit our building site for the children's village, 'Home Joseph 1'. Jakob had invited us to his house on the mountain for coffee. It wasn't far, just about twenty minutes, as he had said on the phone. His son Constantin, who was still at school in TCV (Tibetan Children's Village) Dharamshala, would wait to escort us. It sounded easy. We arrived at the agreed place on time and climbed up the relatively steep hill behind Constantin. There was no path, or at least no visible one. The only route available would lead you through a lot of scree, ancient trees and open areas with huge rocks on which hundreds of pinned Tibetan flags could be seen. As a sign of the many mystical and mysterious places of power, the flags lined the path with magnificent views of the Kangra Valley far below. At another 'place of power', the small path turned and we looked up at the 6,000-metre peaks of the Dhauladhar, which is also known as the 'White Range'. Just beyond are Zanskar, Ladakh and the Tibetan homeland, right on the border with China!

I had bought a chocolate cake in McLeodganj as a surprise for the lady of the house. I balanced it up the steep path with one hand, holding on to rocks and branches with the other. An hour went by. We passed by a small Indian farmhouse twice, and to our relief, we found it was fenced in. The guard dogs are known to be very aggressive towards strangers; not only do they bark terribly but they also defend their territory fiercely. As always, I had my pepper spray with me for such attacks, and, of course, I had taken a rabies vaccination as a precaution. Despite knowing Constantin, they still barked in a threatening manner.

I remember my son Andreas asking a little cautiously whether there were any snakes around. Constantin replied with a short 'Yes, sometimes!' and that further raised our pulse rates.

My chocolate cake now looked like a doughnut that had been knocked over several times. It was very hot and the sun was melting the chocolate faster by the minute. I even had to drop it a couple of times, or else I would have lost my balance and fallen. It was an ordeal, but I had already learned one thing from the Tibetans: 'Never give up'. So I carried my deformed chocolate with me. After about an hour and a half, we reached the top of the mountain. Huge black shepherd dogs ran towards us, barking wildly but wagging their tails happily to greet Constantin. What I didn't understand was why the dogs had metal collars around their necks, about 10 cm wide. I would learn later on what they were for.

Jakob had heard the barking and was coming towards us. His son, who had struggled to pull us up, gave him a brief but rather contemptuous look to describe our condition. Well, we certainly weren't the best climbers. And Constantin was right. He walked this route every day to school and, of course, back home. Sometimes, he was allowed to use one of the two pack animals that roamed freely up there. But then they were tied up outside the school all day, and they didn't like that at all. For Jakob's family, who had been walking up and down this path in the Himalayas for almost four decades, even late at night, this was something quite normal. But for us, untrained city dwellers, it was a real challenge!

The table was already set under the covered porch of the typical Indian U-shaped farmhouse. Felicitas had baked a wonderful chickpea cake and—what a surprise—there was the Austrian 'Jakobs coffee', easily recognisable from the coffee can—and it was, above all, a nice play on words. I was ashamed of my dented chocolate cake, but they thanked me with friendly smiles. In Tibet, it is the willingness to make the other happy that is most valued.

The children of the Jakob family greeted us just as warmly and disappeared again to go and play on the small platform where a miniature basketball court had been set up. I wondered what would happen if the ball fell over the steep slope. The children at the SOS Children's Village in the valley below would surely be delighted.

Jakob took us for a walk around his property. Behind the house was a chicken coop woven from willow. He told us that a few days ago, the mountain leopard had broken into the cage and killed all the chickens. My son asked why he didn't shoot it, to which Jakob wisely replied that the leopard had been there long before he had arrived, so he had a right to the few chickens. Two packhorses were grazing relatively freely, and there were two monkeys in another wire shed; Jakob explained that they could attack. They would get their bread of charity here. A huge tin roof had been installed so that rainwater could be collected in a large cistern for drinking purposes, and electricity was generated by a generator. He said they went to bed early and got up early again, often surrounded by chickens, given they weren't eaten by the leopards in their sleep.

I couldn't believe my eyes—up there where fox and leopard say good-night to each other, Jakob had built three tree houses in the few remaining trees. I asked him curiously what he needed them for. He replied with a laugh: 'These tree houses have some great advantages. No woman climbs up there. I'm alone there and nobody bothers me!' But who knows. Maybe the fact that he can connect to the SOS Children's Village Wi-Fi and surf for free on his laptop also played a part in his decision to be up there!

We enjoyed the breathtaking view in peace and quiet. Felicitas served Jakob his coffee. I smoked the pipe I had brought with me and Andreas played with a young sheepdog. The big dogs with the thick tin collars had gathered around us. Felicitas must have realised that I didn't quite understand the point of these unusual and certainly uncomfortable collars. But like everything else up in the mountains, the collars had a practical purpose. Over the past thirty years, the mountain leopard had taken and killed more than twenty dogs. Its hunting pattern was always the same: it grabbed the dog by the neck from behind and dragged it away! They had learned from Tibetan mountain nomads that this tin neck collars would make it impossible for the leopard to drag the dogs away, and so far, it had worked. Still laughing, Jakob remarked that he was now working on a collar for the chickens.

Felicitas spotted my pepper spray, which I always kept attached to my belt. She wanted to know if she could have it. I was used to giving away my pepper spray to locals before leaving for home. 'For the leopard?' I asked with a grin. 'No,' Felicitas replied seriously. 'They're too fast. But the Himalayan bears have become very aggressive lately. Last winter a huge bear broke into the kitchen at night and ate all the food.' Felicitas's voice trembled at the memory of that scary night. Separated only by a thin door, she had sat in the bedroom trembling for her life.

Andreas and I looked at each other again, eyes wide, silent and questioning. Jakob and his family didn't 'live in nature', they 'lived with it', in exemplary harmony. I had never seen such joyful people living contentedly in such beautiful surroundings.

I had met Tiki, the adopted daughter, on and off on several occasions across several years. She was a beautiful Tibetan girl. At some point, she moved to Vienna to study but eventually abandoned her studies for love. Together with an African man whom she had fallen in love with, she opened a pub in Vienna. Unfortunately, the pub became a well-known drug dealing centre and the police closed it down. Soon, Tiki became the mother of a beautiful boy who was born with Tibetan features and the hair of his African father. After a while, the father left both the mother and son.

Much later, Jakob told me that some twenty years after her escape, Tiki, with an Austrian passport, was granted a long-awaited entry permit to Tibet to reunite with her biological parents. Just two weeks before she arrived in Lhasa, her old Tibetan home, her father, whom she had not seen for twenty years, died. What a tragedy!

Now, Jakob's son, who had dragged us up the long mountain path to his parents' house in the mountains many years ago, and his sister, the younger adopted Tibetan daughter, will be doing a catering internship in our restaurant. I'm looking forward to returning some of their great hospitality.

8

At the Tibetan Children's Villages

Tsewang Jeshe is the director of the eighteen Tibetan Children's Villages in India. Smiling happily, he greeted us on the steep steps leading up to the SOS-run Tibetan Childrens Villages (TCV) headquarters. He was holding white *khatas*, thin silk scarves traditionally given to guests and friends as a welcome gift. I must be having about a hundred of these at home. I make it a point to carry back the tokens of great hospitality of my beloved Tibetan friends.

Mr Tsewang invited us into his small office. The sparse walls were decorated with photographs of well-known Tibetan personalities, including the Dalai Lama's sister Jetsun Pema (known as Amala, the mother of Tibet), who is still president of all the TCVs, and the Austrian founder of SOS Children's Villages, Hermann Gmeiner. Of course, there was also a photo of the Dalai Lama himself with Heinrich Harrer. All the rooms were dominated by a large picture of the Dalai Lama placed directly above the desk.

It filled me with pride to see so many people from my native Austria in His Holiness's circle. We were served tea as the manager of TCV Dharamshala and his long-time friend Wangdoo joined us.

I explained to Mr Tsewang the reason for our visit. This time I was not carrying money for new facilities. Instead, I had financed the trip of a film crew. It was very important for me to draw Europe's attention to the fate and problems of Tibetan children in northern India. There was hardly anyone in Europe who knew about how these children dangerously escaped and crossed the snow-covered mountains of the Himalayas to get a good education among their peers in the SOS Children's Villages.

These were my thoughts and ideas. Whether Carola, the director, and her cameraman would be able to realise them was out of my hands. However, we had been working hard and had collected some very useful footage. What was missing was footage of the Tibetan childrens home. Later, I wanted to talk to the Dalai Lama. Of course, I knew how difficult that would be. But if you don't ask, you've already lost. So I simply asked Tsewang Jeshe to arrange a meeting with him, putting it as politely and amicably as I could by adding 'if at all possible'. I didn't want to put him under too much pressure.

In the meantime, our cameraman had completed all the technical preparations and the 'director' asked Jeshe for an interview. It turned out to be a pretty good and detailed interview. Jeshe didn't mince his words and spoke at length about his work and his plans for the future of SOS Children's Villages. However, he was particularly concerned about a new problem that had arisen. Due to stricter border controls by the Chinese, but mainly because of corrupt Nepalese officials, it had become increasingly difficult for the children to cross the

Chinese border to the SOS Children's Villages. Unfortunately, he could not find a remedy. The fight against corruption seemed to be getting harder in Tibet too.

It seemed doubtful whether our planned documentary would be able to make a difference, but it was certainly worth a try. Towards the end of the interview, Carola kept trying to bring the conversation back to the Dalai Lama, but Jeshe skilfully evaded her questions and, above all, avoided making a concrete commitment to an interview with His Holiness. Anna, the director, looked at me with big questioning eyes while Jeshe tried to smile away his embarrassment.

I was much more relaxed about it all. Up there, you have to believe that something will work. And it usually does. I had learnt that much from my previous visits to Tibet and the many meetings I had had with the Dalai Lama. Each time I received a confirmation of the meeting, I feared it would get cancelled. The fear of having travelled all the way from Europe only to get nothing at last created enormous pressure. If you talked about such a meeting too early, it could cost you dearly. It was as if you owed everyone an explanation. Otherwise, you would be labelled a 'busybody', a 'liar', a 'failure' or even just a 'show-off'. In any case, these were the thoughts that tormented a westerner like me most at the time.

It was only when I realised how many people wanted to meet this eighty-year-old monk, how many dreamed of an audience with him, that I realised how selfish and stubborn I was. I had to take a more relaxed view. If it happens, that's wonderful—if it doesn't happen, that's okay too. I reminded myself: *How important are you in the long line of film stars, presidents and kings? Do not forget the Tibetans who walk for weeks from almost inaccessible mountain valleys to meet their living God for once in their lives.*

Of course, my fellow travellers were miles away from such thoughts. They wanted to bring back a good story. That was the reason why they came all the way and that was why they were fighting for their story and pushing through. What else could it be for—they were doing their job and everyone, including me, understood that. I simply thought to myself: *Let go, relax ... it'll happen ... you'll get your interview.*

Last September, Helmut Kutin, successor to SOS founder Hermann Gmeiner and president of SOS Children's Villages International from 1986 to 2012, came to visit. He was, of course, received by the Dalai Lama. I remember a conversation we had when I went to meet Kutin in Tyrol. He told me about an argument he had had with the Dalai Lama and described a completely different, apparently unknown side of this living God. With unimaginable strength and power, the Dalai Lama had defended his point of view in a heated discussion to convince Kutin of its correctness. Of course, at first look, such behaviour might appear to be inconsistent with the image we Europeans have of this 'monk', who always seems to be happy and up for a joke. However, if you think about it, you will see that it is also part of the task of Tibetan Buddhism's ultimate spiritual teacher to cope with uncomfortable situations and successfully advocate his point of view—aggressively if need be.

Advocating the rights of minorities has never been easy. The Dalai Lama also has to protect his people and fight for their freedom, not with deadly weapons but with the wisdom of words. This comes from a long tradition in Tibet. Through mock debates, even the child monks have to learn how to use strong hand movements, backed up by clapping and loud words, to persuade their opponent to accept their point of view.

Sometimes, I have witnessed such debating sessions myself, sitting in the courtyards of the monasteries high in the Himalayas at sunset as I watched the monks go on with their practice. I didn't understand the words, but the wild gestures, accompanied by expressive grimaces and loud shouting, were no less than a language—and that too a clear one!

Such sessions were always conducted under the guidance and strict observation of older monks. When the argument was over, they would start again, this time the roles getting reversed. The previous winner would suddenly find himself in the defensive position. In this way, both parties learned that there were always two different points of view on the same issue and that these needed to be weighed against each other. What I found particularly beautiful and reassuring at the same time was how the opponents disappeared back into their monastic hermitages after the 'training course', holding hands affectionately. There was so much in it for our European politicians to learn from considering how shamefully they debate.

It is said that the Dalai Lama passed many of these rhetorical examinations with great success in his youth. This training certainly stood him in good stead as he fought for the future of his people. 'Never give up' was the motto of the Tibetans in exile. The right words can do more than any battle. That was the point of the exercise.

Soon, Lobsang Tsomo arrived. She gave me a happy and inviting smile. She was the secretary of the director of TCV, Tsewang Jeshe, and I'd been in close contact with her for many years. She would accompany us to the baby home. We bid our goodbyes as I promised my two friends that I would visit them again soon. Together with the cameraman and director, we first had to climb the endless steps to the TCV. On our way, we passed by houses and could see freshly washed clothes left hanging outside to dry.

Remember, Tibetan children must wash and iron their own clothes! Early in the morning you can see them kneeling on the floor, rubbing their clothes vigorously with soft soap and brushes—just like our grandmothers used to do. The clothes are then rinsed with fresh water from the nearby well and hung out to dry.

Sometimes, we passed by the houses very closely, so much so that I peered curiously through one of the small windows and saw a boy reading one of his school books intently. A housewife greeted me warmly from the open door. She was wearing a beautiful Tibetan costume that I have always admired. The caregivers in the children's villages are not allowed to wear modern clothes—they want to portray an image of Tibetan homeland for the children. Of course, this does not go without controversy. At one lunch, Lobsang whispered to me, sounding mildly critical, that she thought it was unfair that all the women had to wear traditional Tibetan dress while the Tibetan men in the children's villages were allowed to work wearing jeans and casual clothes. So, there is still a lot of work to be done in terms of emancipation on different levels.

The baby home itself is separated from the rest of the large compound by a large, barred door. Walking through it we entered a small courtyard, where we saw a large shady tree right in the middle. In the sunny courtyard, we spotted two drying cots. But there was no sign of the expected baby cries. On the contrary, it was very quiet. The babies were probably sleeping. Only one girl, about three years old, was playing alone in the yard with small round stones. We found out later that the child's name was Dolma. I took one of the Josef balloons I had brought with me and blew it up into a big red ball. What unfolded next was exactly what I had hoped for: Dolma's eyes lit up with joy and she ran to me with her arms wide open. I handed her the balloon with an encouraging smile and started to play tag with her using the balloon. She picked up the tricks of the game in no time.

While we were playing, one of the mothers at the baby home told me that Dolma had only been there for two days and that she had gone through traumatic experiences in her short life. Tibetan men had carried her all the way there over the endless mountains of fate. Her mother had been raped by Chinese soldiers, and Dolma, the result of the atrocious act, was now growing up in the baby home. It was the express wish of her mother, who still lived in Chinese-occupied Tibet. It's not that she didn't love her child—the truth was far from it. She wanted her child to be educated in the centuries-old Tibetan culture in Dharamshala. And this was the only way she could prevent her child from being re-educated by the Chinese occupiers. In return, she made peace with the fact that she might never see her daughter again. Being too old to change, she stayed with her family and the other children in the homeland occupied by Chinese soldiers.

This moving story brought tears to my eyes. Where are they, the human rights activists of our world, preoccupied with nonsensical gender regulations, delayed and distracted by woolly emancipation activities? This is where the real problems lie and such issues are much more complicated. And nobody dares to come up with a solution.

Lost in thought, I had almost forgotten about little Dolma. She was bored by now, but she noticed the change in my demeanour. She grabbed me by the arms and made it clear that she wanted to play with me again. So we resumed playing with the balloon. No foreign language can stop you from communicating with a child. Dolma squealed with delight when she caught the balloon, but as soon as she dropped it, she wrinkled her forehead. As soon as a young Tibetan boy intervened and tried to take the balloon from her, a small argument broke out. I nipped it in the bud and simply blew up a second balloon—a red Josef balloon of course—to avoid further arguments.

Dolma seemed very happy with the solution. She had got hold of the 'new' balloon and suddenly stood in front of me with it, bowing with gratitude and the most beautiful child's smile I had ever seen. Then she proudly walked back into one of the houses with her present tucked under her arm.

I took advantage of the quiet time to find a spot under the biggest tree and rest my eyes. One of my former travel companions runs one of the most beautiful and successful children's hotels in Austria. She is the mother of two young children who are lucky enough to have grown up in this first-class hotel. In a country where inexhaustible social wealth allows mothers to receive a salary for almost three years without having to go to work, it has become possible for mothers to take care of their children during the most important initial years of their lives—to be there for their children when they need them, to tell them the stories of their parents, to sing songs of past generations and to tell them about their grandparents. A mother's love is and remains the greatest happiness a child can experience.

At least, that's the theory. Unfortunately, reality often fails to keep up. As soon as these European kids can be dropped off at a state-subsidised crèche, many mothers take advantage of this generous social facility. Instead of taking care of their children themselves, they often drop them off early in the morning at these state-run 'collection centres' to avoid too much 'stress'.

Sometimes these stressed-out mothers simply forget to pick up their children even by late afternoon. It seems doubtful to me that the embarrassing phone calls to remind them will change anything in the future. My colleagues in the catering industry keep telling me that their restaurants and cafés are packed during the day with state-funded mothers on maternity leave who have 'dropped off' their babies. That can't be the aim of modern maternity protection.

While I was daydreaming, my film crew had finished filming outside and had gone inside to film the babies napping. They lay in their beds looking like little angels, carefree and innocent, often in pairs, cuddled up close to one another. Unfortunately, it was inevitable that some of the babies would wake up. Perhaps a little frightened, they watched us sleepily. The boys were the first to sit up in their cribs. They started dancing and jumping around to get our attention. It didn't take long for all the babies to wake up.

Soon there were about twenty of them, happily vying for our attention in their childish, innocent way. Admirably calm and loving, the two baby home mums tried to bring some calm to the chaos. They had little success, but we can never be certain because they were both speaking to them in the local language. It also seemed that the children were simply amused by the presence of strangers. I'm not sure whether all the children there could understand the local language, for there are too many regional dialects in this vast country.

In the middle of the small room, a child decided to use the wooden floor as a toilet. The mother, who was around, scolded the three-year-old boy. It worked; he quickly fetched a mop and tried to clean up his little shameful act.

As visitors from affluent Europe who had grown up with tonnes of used paper nappies and absorbent Pampers, we were naturally a little disgusted. But I also remember my mother teaching me the way to the chamber pot. In those days, washing cloth nappies was a tedious but natural task for our great mothers. Washing lines and clean laundry were the pride of every mother back in the day, and more important than many a battle over gender and women's rights.

Anna and her cameraman David were delighted with the wonderful footage they had managed to capture from their visit to the baby home: a bouncing red-cheeked boy struggling for attention, a crying dark-haired girl, the boy who got scolded by the mother, and much more. We had disturbed the babies' naps, but the stay-at-home mums managed to calm them down.

The children's toys were neatly organised in a separate room. On the wall, we could see a large painted sheet with drawings stuck on it; a kindergarten aunt had brought back the artworks from Austria, all of which were gifts from her Austrian children. Like kindergartens in our part of the world, the children's rooms in Tibet too were filled to the ceiling with toys.

I know that many European visitors bring mountains of old toys for the kids. But I also know that many of these toys are passed on to places in the far-flung villages of the Himalayas where children still play with hand-carved dolls and colourful stones, as has been happening for centuries in such places. I also brought with me a suitcase full of teddy bears and stuffed animals. The housemothers immediately distributed these 'treasures' to the children who had tears of joy in their eyes. We spent some time talking to the housemothers about their experiences and adventures with the children in their care. They start teaching the kids fundamental values such as respect, tolerance and charity from an early age. These virtues are the cornerstones of the lives of these homeless yet peaceful mountain people. At the same time, these virtues are often sought in vain in our latitudes and, in fact, are being increasingly forgotten!

Over time, I have also witnessed some changes in myself. For a long time, I came to give gifts and donations. This time, I was coming to escape my stressful life and get some time away from the restaurant; to absorb the ancient wisdom and lifestyle of the Tibetans; and to combine it with the heritage and culture of my parents and grandparents. Strengthened in this way, I could then plunge back into the brutal, wasteful world of European affluence.

But I had my doubts. I was not sure whether my world was really the right one. Did I keep coming back because I wanted to help, or was it because I wanted to relax? I still don't have the answers. But there is a strange, recurring, deep feeling, a memory of having been one of them in a previous life.

Thoughtfully, and without many words, we left that unique place together, where, day after day, people are painstakingly, carefully and lovingly trying to prepare even the youngest members of an ancient, dying culture for the great battle of survival. May you never give up, Tibet!

9

The Himalayas Are Burning!

We ended our visit to the SOS Children's Village satisfied with the quality of the footage. It was time to go back to the Tibetan guest house in the Himalayas.

While my companions rested for a while, I decided to visit one of the five large Buddhist monasteries in the valley. Almost all of those had undergone extensive renovation in recent years and some had even been rebuilt. I visited the sites time and again, observing and photographing the progress. Now that most of the work was finished after decades of construction and radiating a Tibetan grandeur, second only to the Potala Palace in Lhasa, I was eager to see them again. I made an addition to my agenda for the day: Sherabling Monastery*, a huge Buddhist monastic university and world-renowned institute.

The view from the window of my room—the golden roofs glistening in the sun on the horizon—dispelled any doubts I might have had about whether it was worth making the long journey. To save at least a little time, I persuaded my jeep driver to take a shortcut through the foothills of the Himalayan cedar forests. He didn't know the way and was obviously worried about taking a potentially unsafe route. Nevertheless, I insisted. I was absolutely sure that I would be able to find this path again if need be. After all, I had been on that route with my Tibetan friends not very long ago.

Unfortunately, things turned out a little differently. I soon discovered that I had taken a wrong turn, the consequences of which almost cost us our lives. It was only when it became steeper and more difficult to drive on the narrow forest road that my driver and I realised that this could not be the right way to the monastery institute. We tried to manoeuvre our way, always keeping an eye on the deep abyss with a few trees. My driver didn't utter a word, but his withering looks said it all. Far down in the valley, we could see the roofs of Sherabling glistening in the sun, but our destination was getting further and further away. It was the beginning of a dangerous odyssey. Were we now to turn around and go back? That didn't seem to be a good plan because neither of us had an answer to the question 'where to?'. The new crossroads that kept appearing confused me more and more. I had no idea which way to go. I gave up and decided to leave our luck in the hands of my driver. At least that would spare me his disapproving looks. But he was undoubtedly right about one thing: we should not have tried to take the 'shortcut'.

On the steep drive down the valley, I closed my eyes, trying to think of one of the many stories told in the monastery guest house over cold Kingfisher beer.

In the past, a lifetime ago or so, there were tigers in the vast forests in the region. But many were driven into Nepal and Bhutan, or into the few nature reserves, or fell victim to the hunting parties of the local kings. There were also stories about hungry wolves and bears coming very close to the farmers during cold winter months and killing their livestock. And then there were the much-feared mountain leopards. In winter, driven by hunger, they still show up in the small Indian villages to get their meals, which mostly consist of dogs, sheep and goats. My friend, the maharaja of Kangra, loves to tell the story of a young mountain leopard that not only regularly prowls around his house just below the Dalai Lama's temple in Dharamshala but also likes to make himself comfortable in an open jeep outside his house.

These stories might sound engaging but are tragedies by the end of the day. Due to the ongoing deforestation and the ever-increasing human population in the territory, it is an unfortunate fact that the increasingly oppressed predators are no longer able to find the space they so desperately need. Acting like a predator, humans have occupied the space of the weaker animals, be it in distant Tibet or the mountainous areas we were covering. It is always the weaker animal that has to submit.

I could see the small clouds of smoke in the mountains when we set off for the monastery. I expected to see campfires in the villages. Unfortunately, I was wrong. As we drove around a huge rock, we realised to our horror that the smoke was the result of a forest fire that was being continuously fanned by the wind. We couldn't believe our eyes. We were in the middle of a terrifying forest fire in the Himalayas! We were surrounded and trapped by smoking embers. I had repeatedly seen reports on television about the devastating wildfires in California, and, of course, I remembered the Australian bushfires of recent years. I had not forgotten about the African bushfires either. But when I found myself in the middle of such a hellish sea of flames, I was immediately overwhelmed.

My driver instinctively stepped on the accelerator. The small forest track was lined with mountains of needles from the giant cedars, and they were just beginning to ignite in the searing heat. How does such a massive wildfire start? I have no idea. But it is often the shards of a discarded bottle that frequently serve as a magnifying glass, and the focused rays of sunlight grow so intense that the dust-dry cedar needles spontaneously ignite. And the light breeze does the rest.

I saw smouldering fires up to 10 metres to the right and left of the road. It was producing a great deal of smoke, obscuring the view. Then I saw flames leaping dangerously high in the air. The road itself was still clear. But what did that mean? After the next turn, everything could be different again. The many small, steep valleys made it difficult to see what was in store for us around the next turn. But we didn't have a choice. There was no way up, so we had to go down the valley. My driver stepped on the gas and sped through the clouds of smoke like James Bond—as far as that expression can be used while traversing the narrow mountain roads.

There was suddenly a clearing! No smoke, no smouldering fires. We stopped, took a deep breath and stared at each other. What should we do? Once again, our eyes captured more than words could convey. We had to keep going on, with the hope that everything would be alright! Again and again, we came across 30–50-metre-long pockets of embers. The only advantage was that the old cedars were very tall, but the branches had just started to sprout. The embers stayed on the ground. Sometimes it would die out for a short time, only to flare up again on a flammable surface. The embers continued to eat their way across the ground like a giant anaconda. Fascinated and frightened at the same time, I hurriedly took out my camera and managed to get a few bad but telling shots as my driver continued to drive the jeep downhill. Then we got lucky—really, really lucky. A little further down the valley, I could see that the fire was dying out. The path, trampled by many walkers, had not caught fire.

Shortly afterwards, we found the right turn and finally reached Sherabling Monastery unharmed. We sat in the jeep for a few minutes, speechless. Being a universal body language, our collective sigh of relief united us in that moment. Such gestures always work, be it in the best or the worst situation that life has in store for us. That sigh from the depths of our souls said more than what a thousand words could have said. We had managed to escape the blazing inferno—together! At last, we smiled at each other with joy. In both our languages, it meant the same thing: 'We were lucky, my friend!'

Now I wonder who would have come to find our charred bodies in the solitude of the Himalayas? 'Missing, kidnapped or hiding as a monk in a Buddhist monastery' would have been the headlines in my homeland.

Once again, I gave the driver a more than generous tip when I bid him adieu. He had not only saved his own life but mine as well.

An accident or illness in the mountains was fatal, for help was often several days away. Over 6,000-metre-high passes would have to be crossed. Both pack animals and human settlements, including medical facilities, were rare. One might think about calling rescue helicopters using mobile phones. While it might be a good idea, it hardly worked in the mountains due to the lack of network coverage. Caution and adequate preparation before undertaking risky treks are the only precautionary aid that works in the region.

We could hear deep gurgling sounds coming from a short distance. They almost seemed like eerie chants from ancient times. Mystical mantras, punctuated by the muffled sounds of Tibetan alphorns and little brass bells. It all had a very hypnotic effect on me. The sounds of long conch shell fanfares, blown repeatedly in between, brought me back to reality. The monks of the monastery had gathered for the daily mass. Despite the many difficulties that had put our lives in danger, we had managed to arrive at the right time for the puja.

My driver stayed by the jeep, smoking a cigarette with relish. I looked enquiringly at the monk at the entrance. And the international 'language without words' worked again. He nodded and I was allowed to enter the huge covered inner hall of the monastery but not without taking off my shoes first. In the courtyard, some young monks were preparing *tsampa* (A Tibetan food) in huge pots. The roasted barley was mixed with equally huge quantities of crumbled biscuits, which another group was tossing in after collecting from small bags. This was a rare luxury treat, so I assumed they had been given an extremely cheap supply of sweets. They paid no heed to expiry dates, and even if there was one mentioned on the label, nobody took it seriously. Edible food meant food; expired did not mean inedible. All that had to be kept in mind was that most Tibetans were vegetarians.

Coming to think of it—how many tonnes of valuable food have we thrown away in our catering business? What a disgrace! All because European food law does not allow us to use it. And then there are the resourceful propagandists who invite us to multi-course gala dinners collected and prepared from food fished out of containers to draw attention to this problem of affluence. How crazy our world is! First, we are bombarded with laws and regulations, then new authorities are created to monitor these European Union (EU) regulations, some of which border on insanity. Unfortunately, using common sense seems to have gone out of fashion. Passing down knowledge and experience from parents and teachers would be more sensible and, above all, cheaper.

I recently read on a Facebook page that huge Chinese shopping temples are being planned in the centre of Lhasa. The photos showed cranes and excavators in Tibet's former Buddhist capital, digging deep trenches in what was once sacred ground. It was the very soil where even a tiny worm used to be carefully saved from getting trampled, keeping in line with the belief that a Tibetan rebirth could be hidden in the smallest of creatures. You can see and admire this philosophy in the epic film *Seven Years in Tibet*.

How quickly the world changes! A hundred years ago, no foreigner was allowed to enter the city of the Dalai Lama. That was a good thing. It would have been much easier to preserve this unique, almost 2,500-year-old culture, and promote and pass on its knowledge for the benefit of future generations. But, once again, short-sighted policy of economic growth has prevailed as the only yardstick for development.

When the Yellow Army entered Lhasa in 1950, the hard-to-reach Tengyeling medical monastery was blown up on a mountain opposite the Potala Palace. The mysterious art of Tibetan medicine and astrology, handed down for generations, had been practised there till then. Everything was for the benefit of the people. Later, the Chinese occupiers banned the production and sale of Tibetan medicine.

But of what use would a cultureless 'shopping temple' be compared to this ancient knowledge? Once again, I understand the Tibetan mothers who prefer to send their children on a dangerous journey over the mountains in order to help them learn the knowledge and value of their culture. Being deeply attached to their tradition, the mothers understand how important it is to preserve this knowledge for humanity.

In the Himalayas, there are women who live with several men—often brothers—and are married to all or some of them. Often, such a woman is the only heir to a mountain farm. Sex is not the reason for this, as the 'spoilt rich man' who lives in luxury might think. The man's work to cultivate the barren fields and protect the herds of yaks and sheep requires this polyandry*.

It is a law of nature that guarantees the survival of the family, tradition and the hard-won fields.

The entrance to the huge main hall of the monastery was draped in flowing cloth. Understandably, the monks didn't want to be disturbed and, of course, I respected that. I could watch them through the dirty windows at the side.

At the front, slightly raised on his golden throne, sat the Rinpoche, the spiritual head of the monastery. He held the Tibetan thunderbolt, the *dorje*, as a symbol of his power and position. Directly behind him, in the centre, was a gigantic, gilded statue of Buddha, perhaps 10 metres high. Finely carved yak butter sculptures were placed at his feet.

Hundreds of smaller Buddha statues adorned the altar. In the front, there was a big offering bowl containing large sums of banknotes. The brass bowls containing with water are said to calm evil spirits. Flanking the Buddha statue on either side were slightly smaller but extremely impressive figurines of Bodhisattvas*, painted in different colours.

An old monk could be seen going from one monk to another, holding a large paper bag and placing banknotes on the table for each of them, according to their rank. I realised that the date was 1 June and it was supposed to be payday! I watched this ceremony for a long time. Stories of Indian idolatry, human sacrifice and mysterious sectarian fairs were running through my mind. But wouldn't these people from Tibet feel the same at a mass in our latitudes? I sneaked away, but not without taking a few good photos—without flash, of course, as I didn't want to disturb anyone.

I returned to the guest house, this time walking along the main road which was quiet and safe. I decided to visit the other monasteries in the area on another occasion, as we were to have dinner with my fellow travellers and Rigo Tulku Rinpoche.

A beautifully painted giant rock in the SOS Children's Village for Tibetan refugees in Bir, Himachal Pradesh, India

Mani stones near the kora site around the Dalai Lama Temple in McLeodganj, Himachal Pradesh, India

Monks waiting to welcome His Holiness the Dalai Lama in Tso Pema, Mandi, Himachal Pradesh

(Clockwise from left): Buddhist monks carrying gifts for the opening ceremony of the Zangdok Palri Phodang Temple; Church of St John in the Wilderness, McLeodganj; Kora site around the temple of the Dalai Lama, McLeodganj

Opening ceremony of the Zangdok Palri Phodang Temple in Rewalsar, Tso Pema, Himachal Pradesh

Statue of Padmasambhava (Guru Rinpoche) in a cave near Rewalsar, Tso Pema, Himachal Pradesh

Author with Tibetan monks in Lhasa, Tibet

Praying in front of a Tibetan altar in McLeodganj, Himachal Pradesh, India

Tailoring facilities for Tibetan refugee girls at the Tibetan Children's Village (TCV) School in Patlikuhal, Kullu Valley, Himachal Pradesh

A student honing his art at Thangka Painting School at TCV School in Patlikuhal

A painting on display in Thangka Painting School

Another student engrossed in his work at Thangka Painting School

Children enjoying a party at 'Home Josef' in Upper TCV, McLeodganj, Dharamshala

Home Josef for the Elderly in Choglamsar, Leh, India; author in the backrow (fourth from left)

Author (in the backrow, third from left) with friends and Tibetan refugee children

The author sponsored an Austrian concert tour of The FreeMenSingers in Tibetan schools in the Himalayas.

A concert at Tibetan old people's home

Author interacting with His Holiness the 14th Dalai Lama in McLeodganj

10

My First Audience

The phone rang and abruptly pulled me out of my thoughts. It was Elisabeth Zimmermann, my favourite 'Tibetan Mother Teresa' from Vienna. This time, she had a very special surprise for me, and it was beyond anything I had ever experienced before. Of course, I was aware that the Dalai Lama was in Austria to take part in a symposium at the magnificent Melk Abbey. What I didn't know was that the Tibetan leader wanted to meet me there for a personal audience to thank me for building my first orphanage in the small Indian mountain village of Suja. I wanted to know when that would be. 'Tomorrow in Melk!' The answer left me speechless. It doesn't happen very often, but I couldn't say a word. I, the rebellious landlord of Linz's Gasthaus Josef, known for my often critical and unpopular statements, was to receive this great honour—I couldn't believe it.

Of course, I had also read in the media how our much-vaunted democratic government was using hypocritical excuses to prevent a reception for the Dalai Lama. Nobody wanted to jeopardise the oh-so-important economic relations with the booming state of China. No one, neither our federal president nor the ruling chancellor, dared to receive the Nobel Peace Prize winner and religious leader of one of the most peaceful nations. How embarrassing for Austria—one of the world's most famous tourist destinations, where hospitality is usually a top priority. Where had it gone—our much-vaunted Austrian hospitality? Had everyone forgotten how we ourselves had fared after the occupation by the Third Reich? After all, the federal president must have experienced that time himself. The fact that I, of all people, had the honour of being received personally by the Dalai Lama was beyond my comprehension.

However, I was preoccupied with a much more mundane question so shortly before the expected audience: What should I wear? Should I wear one of my Tibetan dresses out of respect for His Holiness? Probably not—it might look ridiculous. Perhaps a black suit? No, I'd rather not. It would be too formal, and besides, I'm not a politician. I took a deep breath and tried not to think of anything for ten seconds. Then, suddenly, the solution was obvious, and I decided to put on our traditional suit, with lederhosen, of course—what else?

Word spread quickly about my audience and a journalist friend from a regional radio station also wanted to be there. Well, why not? I was ready to meet His Holiness.

Long before the appointed time, I stood in the entrance hall of Melk Abbey, watching the hustle and bustle of the many onlookers and visitors. Suddenly, I couldn't believe my eyes! The then federal chancellor and his partner were actually walking past me! Closely followed, in unprecedented unity, by his supposedly hated right-wing arch-enemy, also accompanied by his wife. Too cowardly to stand behind the fate of the

Tibetan people and express this in a public state reception, they sneaked into the secret audience of His Holiness to greet the number one public enemy hated by China. I had caught the four of them beaming with joy and holding hands with their partners as they emerged through a back door. I rushed to the waiting official car and left.

Shortly afterwards, I was invited into an ornate room in the monastery, sat down in one of the waiting chairs and waited. Austrian state police searched me very carefully for weapons, but I was allowed to keep my camera.

Finally, the Dalai Lama entered the room. Smiling and greeting me in a friendly manner, he took my hand and led me forward, kicking his flip-flop sandals off his bare feet and sitting down on the velvet-covered chair in the meditation seat. I couldn't stop myself from scrutinising him somewhat rudely, fascinated by his charisma and unable to take my eyes off him. For the first time in my life, I was face-to-face with the living God of the Tibetan people. 'Ask me,' he invited me to talk to him. He had clearly sensed my embarrassment.

The unexpected invitation to talk to him caused my thoughts to crash and swirl wildly. I thought of the Tibetan children in my orphanages in the Himalayas, who, in addition to Tibetan, Indian and Chinese, spoke better English than I did. And now I was going to talk to one of the most widely travelled, one of the longest-serving heads of state in the world?

The day after my audience with His Holiness, a reception with German Chancellor Angela Merkel was announced in the press. Shortly afterwards, the Dalai Lama was to receive a prestigious award from US president Barack Obama—I thought I was watching the wrong film.

His Holiness recognised my nervousness and spoke first. He asked me, 'How many times have you been to Dharamshala, and how long have you been working on your project. He also wanted to thank me 'for my service and generosity to his people'. The Dalai Lama spoke in an English that I found I could keep up with—it gave me courage. Even on my first trip to Ladakh with Leo, my police friend who had been on several UN peacekeeping missions, I found that the people in the mountains spoke mostly incomprehensible 'Indian English'. They often substituted words with their own language when they weren't sure about it—similar to how I got by with my modest knowledge of the English language. The Tibetan and Indian hill tribes often understood me better than Leo despite the perfect English that he had learnt at school.

I started becoming braver and a little more confident. So, I replied with a counter-question and asked His Holiness about how he felt in Austria and how he liked it.

'Oh yes, very well, Austria is a small country. It's almost like Tibet—the same population, high mountains and wonderful people,' he replied, assuring me that was enjoying his visit.

I was completely unprepared for a question-answer session. Why hadn't I thought of it? I didn't know myself. Perhaps there was too little time, or perhaps the joy of meeting the Dalai Lama in person had made me forget all that.

I gathered the courage to ask him how he found the situation in Tibet and China. 'Everything takes time,' the Dalai Lama said. He added that he too would like to see some progress for the Chinese people. It was interesting to note that millions of Chinese people converted to Buddhism in recent years. It was a typically positive response. However, given that the Chinese government itself was feverishly searching for a state religion to underpin its political path, it seemed rather unlikely that the Dalai Lama would be accepted as a religious leader.

I remember the many demonstrations organised by the Falun Gong sect in China's major cities. The Chinese government had banned them because they were supposedly a threat to the Chinese way. I wished His Holiness that may the path of his Buddhist heritage be more successful than that of the Falun Gong sect. One of the most famous lamas of the God Kings who ruled Tibet, Ngawang Lobsang Gyatso, prophesied: 'Only when steel carriages and iron birds appear over Tibet will Buddhism spread throughout the world!'

It was a sad prophecy that came true when the Chinese army invaded Tibet. As is so often the case, there is light where there is shadow, and thus there is a glimmer of hope for Tibet's old and mystical religion.

The prophecy indeed became a reality. Rarely has a religion like Buddhism spread so widely across the globe. In our hectic and pressured times, more and more people seem to find peace in the philosophy of Buddhism. They are restless people in search of happiness, just like me.

Where are our religious leaders with their thousands of years of knowledge? Why is Christianity failing to provide a sense of succour and comfort? The Dalai Lama confirmed my thoughts by going on to say that he didn't understand why so many westerners wanted to become Buddhists, since every culture has its own religion, which should also be cultivated and studied.

He went on to explain to me that the West has been raised for generations on the ideas of materialism, achievement and capitalism. There is an increasing demand to achieve and move higher, faster and further. 'No wonder you can't find peace. We Tibetans have been studying spiritual science for centuries. Only those who have nothing are without any worries and can thus devote themselves fully to the search for happiness.

They don't think there's any point in jumping from one faith to another, saying "it doesn't work". The monks of Western religions are called to "take care of their people".'

I agreed with him, not knowing that I would also join the Buddhist path shortly before completing my book.

Tenzin Taklha, His Holiness's secretary, politely informed us that we had already exceeded our scheduled time and that other guests were waiting.

His Holiness had given me a khata as a gift and I requested him to sign it for me. No matter how embarrassing it may have seemed at the time, today I treasure that scarf.

I said goodbye with a deep bow, folded my closed hands in greeting, and walked backwards and thoughtfully out of the room, happy as if I had just been spared the death penalty. The journalists were waiting outside. They wanted me to describe my impressions. I extended them a favour.

What a pity! Now I would have to be alone with myself and my thoughts for a while.

11

The Concert in the Himalayas

Once again, dance and music became the order of the day in my pub 'Josef'. The FreeMenSingers with Andi Gabauer as bandleader rocked our pub. Many regulars came because everyone loved their music. Afterwards, we thanked them for the good music over a mug of beer and talked about my 'Josef Tibet Project'. We also discussed about my travels in the mountains of northern India and about the many Tibetan children who had fled across the snow-clad mountains to their living god, the Dalai Lama.

Gabauer finally said that he thought it was great and that he too would like to go on a trip to visit the monks and the Tibetan refugee children. Of course, he had no idea that this request would spontaneously trigger a whole series of fantastic ideas in my head. I had to get one of them off my chest straight away: 'What do you think about a concert tour in the Himalayas to the Tibetan Children's Villages?' Without pausing for breath, I continued: 'Just you and your three guitars? It wouldn't be so complicated. Let's do it like this: I'll pay for your flight and accommodation. You'll have to pay for your own food! That would be something! I'm serious—just think about it!'

The three musicians looked at each other in amazement. But they didn't have to think for long. To my great surprise, they replied with a unanimous 'Why not?' We were a funny and not quite sober group of men. I had to laugh, and it would become contagious. Still, I was sure it would just become another spontaneous pub story and no one would talk about it the next day.

But it did not happen so. The three lads stuck to their decision and remained enthusiastic about our adventure in the Himalayas! So off we went to northern India, to the Tibetan refugee children, to my orphanages and to my friends, the monks. We were hopeful of seeing the Dalai Lama. We decided not to bring with us material gifts but music and joy from Austria. What an exciting project! Soon the planning began.

I remember an old friend, Dagulda—an entertainer, that too a great one. He was a student of Marcel Marceau, the undisputed master of French pantomime. Although I had not been in touch with him in recent years, I rang him on the spur of the moment. 'Hello, this is Günter from Linz … the landlord of the 'Josef' … do you remember me? Dagulda, my old friend, I need you … for something very special!' I jumped to the point at once. 'Would you like to travel with us to Tibet? We need you and your skills to entertain the Tibetan refugee children in the Himalayas.'

He didn't answer immediately, but I could feel his 'pantomime approval' through the phone. Or it could be that my incessant stream of words had left him no time to reply. So I just kept on talking. 'There's no fee, but I'll pay for the flight and the room.' There was silence on the phone for a few seconds before I heard a determined 'OK, I'm in!' All that remained now for the trip were formalities. Dagulda was on board. I felt like Yul Brynner in the Hollywood Western *The Magnificent Seven* when he sought out his six best friends, all experienced gunslingers, and asked them to join him in fighting a feared gang that was terrorising an entire village of poor farmers.

Now I needed an audio specialist. The loudspeakers in the schools were old and croaking. I remembered the fiasco at the opening of my Home Josef orphanage. We had our 'Top Josef DJ Werner'. A quick phone call and I had him on board, or rather on the plane.

The project was not only complicated but it was also becoming increasingly expensive. So we had to market our project a bit, and for that, we needed more partners, at least a cameraman and a photographer.

Peter, the owner of a 'one-man film studio', had already done some filming for a regional broadcaster. It made sense to ask him first and see if I could persuade him. He asked me for a little time to think about it. But he came with a go-ahead the very next day, making a request that was easy to fulfil. He wanted his wife to come along. She was a nursery-school-teacher and the perfect companion—it couldn't have been better.

It didn't take long to convince Horst, a well-known photographer for a major Austrian newspaper. My Kiwanis friend Joe heard about our plans and didn't miss the opportunity to come along with a Kiwanis flag, thousands of balloons and a donation. Brigitte, a dear friend, wished to see her Tibetan goddaughter, and thus joined our big and colourful group. Soon there were fourteen of us who set off on the long journey to North India in the Himalayas with the mission of bringing joy to others.

We said goodbye to our Austrian friends with a big party in the 'Josef Gastgarten', with all the proceeds going to the Tibetan children. Off we went by plane to India!

Unfortunately, domestic flights in India are very expensive. So, I arranged for a small bus and we set off on the estimated ten-hour journey to the first children's village of a Tibetan thangka painting school in the Kullu Valley, near the foothills of the western Himalayas.

The planned ten hours turned into fifteen agonising hours due to the bad roads and the many stops for my travelling companions to pee. Each stop was a battle of 'man versus luggage'. The bus was very small, and we had to stow our luggage in the middle of the bus. Every time we got off the bus, we had to climb over the coats, bags and presents lying all over the bus. Each stop in this chaos usually lasted more than thirty minutes. As I was always urging people to hurry, I soon became rather unpopular as the group's hectic driver.

Of course, there were good reasons behind my urge to hurry. If we didn't arrive before sunset, we wouldn't have time to get to the nearby Tibetan children's village and that would upset the whole schedule. I was also sure that the children at the school would be eagerly awaiting our arrival. But luck was on our side once again. Somehow, we managed to reach our destination just before nightfall.

Though sweaty and tired from the endless journey, I urged my friends to give their first performance. So, we got off the cramped bus and tuned up our instruments. Dagulda had already changed into his clown costume on the bus. So with just a bit of paint on his nose, he was ready to go.

In the huge, dilapidated school in Patlikuhal, around 200 Tibetan students were waiting for a very special concert experience. The FreeMenSingers kicked things off and soon everyone was swaying, clapping and singing enthusiastically to mark the start of our planned Himalayan concert tour. The happiness in the children's eyes made us forget our long tiring journey. Dagulda's comedy show was new to us as well. It was engaging and funny at the same time. We couldn't stop laughing and had to hold our stomachs to keep from falling off our chairs.

When our hour-long performance, the premiere of our colourful group of jugglers and musicians from Austria, was over, the director, who was a long-time friend of mine, stood up and announced a performance by his students. This was for us.

The children from the thangka painting school wanted to surprise us with a Tibetan dance performance to thank us for the concert. About thirty young people, dressed in beautiful old Tibetan costumes, came on stage and sang traditional songs. Seeing them dance and perform for us made us very emotional.

You must give to receive. That's what my father taught me when I was a young innkeeper. He probably meant that if I cooked well and learnt how to be an enthusiastic host, the guests would come of their own accord. This time, what we brought to the table was joy and happiness through music and cheerfulness. On the very first day, that joy and gratitude came back a hundredfold. It was then that I realised that only those who learn the art of giving can truly enjoy the blissful feeling of joy.

It was late at night when we finally arrived at our guest house. Although everyone was dead tired, we met on the balcony of the lodge high above the Kullu Valley for a quick drink. Despite our tiredness, it turned into a real premiere party. Andi and his band played the best songs from their extensive repertoire on their guitars until late into the night.

Early the next day we travelled to the small village of Bir, close to the huge SOS Children's Village in Suja, which is home to around 2,000 Tibetan refugee children.

Our arrival had already been announced and the huge hall was packed. It is not every day that the children find an opportunity to see European guests perform live. 'Kiwanis Joe' had his hands full once again, blowing up around 200 balloons with his powerful lungs and releasing them from a gallery above the hall as a surprise for the children watching. This resulted in a huge commotion and a fight for the balloons. The remaining 500 balloons were then simply handed out uninflated, but even these were hotly contested. The FreeMenSingers were really trying—you could see it in their eyes, the joy and passion with which they were working their strings.

Music, of course, is a global language. But we were surprised to know that the children in the mountains knew several international songs and sang along so enthusiastically. Dagulda also went full throttle and had the children in stitches with his comic jokes.

The entire hall with about 2,000 children laughed and stamped their feet with joy. I was standing at the back of the hall and had tears in my eyes—real tears of joy. It was good to see happy children.

Before dinner, we all sat on the terrace of the guest house and talked to each other about the concert and the children. Every one of us was indescribably happy and satisfied.

My friend Rigo Tulku Rinpoche had invited the entire entourage to dinner at his monastery. When we had finished our meal, Rigo asked us if we would like to play for his monks in the monastery. It was a great offer and of course a great honour. The only question was when. Our schedule was pretty tight, and we were kind of booked out. 'Well, now—

right now!' came out of the mouth of the always friendly and smiling monk as he looked at us questioningly.

So now we needed flexibility, and we had it. It was fantastic. Almost 200 monks were already waiting in the assembly hall of the Tibetan monastery. Rigo had obviously assumed that I wouldn't refuse his request. All the Buddhist clergy were eager to see what would happen. I am sure this was the first Western concert in the lives of most of the monks there.

So the FreeMenSingers grabbed their guitars and off they went: *'Yellow Submarine'* by the Beatles, hard rock and romantic songs were played. It was a joy to see young and old monks of all religious ranks smiling happily, swinging their clean-shaven heads from side to side and swaying along. Countless mobile phones were held aloft to capture the concert on video. I don't think any band in the world has ever played to such an enthusiastic crowd of monks! The first thing that comes to mind is Johnny Cash's gig at Folsom Prison, although there are few parallels.

At the end of the performance, Rigo Tulku thanked us profusely and invited us to his huge monastery to attend the 'morning mass' the next day.

Unfortunately, we were late again. Getting up early just wasn't our thing. Moreover, we were night owls. Even from a distance, we could hear the muffled gurgling sounds of the monks praying in the puja*.

As always, the chanting was drowned out by drums and Tibetan alpine and conch horns. Rigo Tulku Rinpoche was seated on his ornate high throne. As we entered the rather dark room carefully and quietly, he gave me a friendly look. A very young monk immediately jumped up and led us to a set table in the middle of the monastery, right next to the praying monks. I could hardly believe my eyes: culinary delights ranging from biscuits, dry fruits, varieties of fresh fruits and tea were waiting for us. The monks had invited us to join them for a sumptuous breakfast. Somehow it all seemed completely surreal. Imagine Mass being celebrated in one of the many beautiful churches and monasteries, and fourteen tourists walking in and starting to eat breakfast during Mass—unthinkable! But we were not afraid to accept the offer. After all, we were hungry. So we enjoyed the breakfast and the 'Buddhist programme' to the full.

We had the opportunity to perform four times in front of about 1,000 to 2,000 Tibetan refugee children. The huge halls were always packed. Werner struggled with the old loudspeaker system each time. What would we have done without him? 'Kiwanis Joe' was predestined, because of his corpulence, to blow up hundreds of Josef balloons before each concert. The reward was the immense gratitude of the children and the realisation of how easy it is to make them happy.

Brigitte, a dear friend of many years, was an astrologer and homoeopath. She was also childless. She had been sponsoring a Tibetan girl for many years and communicated with her regularly by email and post. She had given me presents for Yolin, the name of her godchild, on several occasions. I was always annoyed about the amount of chocolate I had to carry with me because, by the time we arrived, it would be completely melted.

This time, however, Brigitte had come herself and we were all looking forward to our first meeting with her almost fifteen-year-old godchild. When a godmother comes to visit, the organisers make sure that the child is brought from the children's villages, some of which are scattered all over India. Brigitte was visibly nervous as the time of her meeting with her godchild approached. 'What am I going to say? I suddenly have motherly duties. Where will she sleep? Can she stay in my room for two days?' she gushed, visibly nervous, shortly before the first meeting.

Soon, everything was forgotten. Yolin arrived and immediately recognised Brigitte. They stood facing each other for a moment. Then they embraced and began to cry.

We were very moved by this encounter and decided to give them some privacy. They must have had a lot to talk about. Yolin was allowed to stay with her godmother for the remaining four days and, of course, she stayed in her room. Brigitte had finally found a daughter.

We heard the stories told by Yolin with great interest. Among other things, she told us that she only had one towel and that she had to wash it on time as there was no second one that could be used. I thought there were so many towels lying around uselessly in the guest house and we didn't even realise it.

Our last evening with Brigitte's godchild was particularly touching and unforgettable. As so often, we sat on the terrace. An incredibly beautiful starry sky twinkled softly above us. Suddenly, Yolin said she wanted to thank us for our hospitality with a song. Never had we heard such a moving song from a young girl who had nothing else to give. It was a very special song that Yolin's mother used to sing to her back in her old homeland in Tibet.

Luckily, I had brought my torch. We listened intently and with great emotion as Yolin sang the ancient Tibetan children's song in the dim light of the torch. The clear Himalayan starry sky, decorated a thousand times over, was the stage; my torch the spotlight; and my friends, more than deeply moved, the concert-goers, as if Leonard Cohen himself was singing his wonderful 'Hallelujah'. We just sat there moved to tears.

The concert at the old-age home, below the Dalai Lama's temple, was equally moving. There were perhaps 150 old

Tibetans living there, many of whom were well-travelled mountain nomads and nuns with sunburnt faces from the high-altitude sun. Some were disabled and had come with antique crutches. They lived in the most basic conditions.

Many tourists from Dharamshala visit the children's villages, but the elderly are sadly forgotten. It is often easier to find sponsors for children. Old people, their fate and their problems go unnoticed. But when you see how lonely people without any financial support, without any way of earning a little money, are happy about a donation of a few euros, you become thoughtful and also depressed at the same time. Reproachful thoughts flashed through my mind once again. It's a shame how carefree we Europeans tend to be with our *Schlaraffenland* prosperity, while others are much worse off.

Under the guise of raising money for Tibetan children, I also donated considerable sums to help build a retirement home for hundreds of old, lonely Tibetan mountain nomads in Ladakh. It opened in the autumn of 2012, just in time for the icy winter. I hope the donors will forgive me. It would not have been possible to raise a single penny for the elderly had we worked under the banner 'We're looking for donations for old Tibetans in the Himalayas'. It would have only worked for raising donations for children.

A small stage was set up in front of the Old People's Home on the hillside using garden benches. The back wall of the stage had been made using sheets hung on a clothesline. Many a curious but not so sprightly resident was carried out on to the street by his fellow residents in front of the makeshift stage so that he too could be a part of this rare experience. I have rarely seen caregivers like the ones I saw then.

Andi Gabauer and the FreeMenSingers began to play so enthusiastically that even the severely handicapped began to groove to the music. We experienced joy, gratitude and enthusiasm—what a privilege!

While the FreeMenSingers were strumming their guitars, my phone rang. It was Mr Wangdoo, the director of TCV, Suja. An old Tibetan friend, he had had just arrived in Dharamshala.

'Günter La [La meaning 'joy'],' he said, 'you must come immediately. Bring your friends. His Holiness the Dalai Lama is at TCV teaching the children. He wants to see you!'

My heart stopped. Of course, I had asked in advance if it was possible to have a brief audience with His Holiness. But, as is so often the case, I had not received a definite promise till then. Too many people wanted to see him. Important and powerful statesmen and religious leaders have always been his guests. They always got the rare honour of a personal audience with him on a priority basis.

But now the Dalai Lama wanted to see us. Now we had our chance! It was time for maybe one last song because some of the residents of the Old People's Home were still dancing in the street to the catchy tunes of the musicians. We had to hurry. Unfortunately, the concert was over far too quickly.

When my friends got to know about the great opportunity, a mad rush ensued. Without any further ado, everyone boarded a bus, and waving a goodbye, we were off to our new destination. Of course, the older concert-goers looked confused and didn't know what was going on. They had no idea why we were leaving in such a hurry. Had they known about the real reason behind our sudden departure, I am sure they would have blessed us. We hurried as, of course, one does not keep the great Dalai Lama waiting.

We urged our bus driver to hurry. Blaring his horn and driving at full throttle, he sped up the steep 5-kilometre road to the TCV. Thousands of Tibetans, mothers with their children, dressed in their finest clothes and traditional costumes, men with beautiful jewellery on their hats, stood along the 1-kilometre access road to the venue. There were also many tourists. Why hadn't we heard about this event before?

It was like a state reception: An endless crowd of people and pilgrims waiting and hoping to see His Holiness. We were able to get past them all because we had a free pass.

Carrying our cameras, we jumped out of the bus. My friend Wangdoo was waiting for us and we followed him to the entrance of the hall.

High Tibetan dignitaries were on guard. His Holiness was already in the Hermann Gmeiner Hall. We had arrived just in time. Over the loudspeakers in the huge hall, we could make out the Dalai Lama's words of wisdom as he spoke to the children. As is usual for the 'ever-cheerful monk', he was in a joking mood. We could always hear the students laughing enthusiastically at the jokes. Wouldn't it be nice to always see similar enthusiasm between students and teachers in our classes?

'Your Holiness,' we heard a Tibetan student ask, 'allow me to ask you a question. There are so many religions, like Christianity, Islam, Hinduism, Judaism, Buddhism and many others. How can I know that I have chosen the right religion?'

'My son,' replied the Dalai Lama, 'this world has so many cultures and religions, so many countries and so many more peoples. Listen to your father's advice and experience, and then listen to your inner voice. Together both will tell you which religion is right for you. All good religions follow the path of love ... Only you can decide which religion you choose for yourself.'

I am always fascinated by how open the Dalai Lama is towards other religions. Many powerful religious leaders try to promote their own religion as the 'only true' one at every opportunity. But this simple monk says to his people: 'Choose for yourselves the religion that you think is right.'

Perhaps it is this practice of tolerance that explains the growing appeal of Buddhism around the world today. For the first time, after many years of being absent from the church, I felt a similar openness towards Buddhism while attending a monthly event organised by a Catholic association called 'Theology on Tap' in our house in Linz. Young, attractive and very committed priests could be seen propagating their faith there, but in a very open way, something I would like to see more often in Christianity.

As the lesson ended, we pushed our way to the front. Everyone wanted to be in the front row. Dagulda still had the clown mask and make-up on his face from his performance at the Old People's Home. It looked funny to us—but what would His Holiness say to him? Andi and his band had their guitars ready. They had written a song for him especially for this moment, *'One Minute of Love'*. What a wonderful song!

Then he finally came out of the hall—the Dalai Lama, slightly bent over, his funny little eyes roaming around as usual. Whom would he look at first? Tsewang Jeshe, the director of TCV, who humbly bowed down, introduced us and briefly explained who we were and what we were doing there. The Dalai Lama smiled at us briefly and thanked us for our concerts. Then he stood amidst us and took my hand and that of Christina, the kindergarten teacher. Beaming with happiness, we looked into Horst's camera. Click, click and click again, everyone wanted to capture the meeting with His Holiness as a precious memory. Then Andi Gabauer got his very personal chance to go on stage with his band. They performed in front of the Dalai Lama, with the premiere of *'One Minute of Love'*. They sang and strummed their guitars like mad fellows.

The Dalai Lama appreciated this and gave them his full attention, with a smile on his face. As always, his time was taken up with other items on his agenda. After all, there were other guests too getting impatient to see him. Right after Andi's performance, a group of beautifully dressed Tibetan women began singing in high, shrill voices. Security guards pushed the crowd to one side. His Holiness's military guards, armed with machine guns, demonstrated that he too has adversaries. The Buddhist leader bowed once more and raised his hands in a gesture of thanks to all the visitors. He bestowed on us one last smile. Then he got into his jeep, accompanied by his escort, and disappeared around the first turn.

After he left, there was absolute silence among the hundreds of people present there. It was as if everyone was replaying the wonderful moment they had just lived. My companions were also beaming as if they had seen the Holy Spirit in person and maybe it really was Him?

The aura of this extraordinary person hung in the air like a clear cloud for a long time. What a feeling of happiness! We sat on the steps of the hall and replayed in our minds the last few minutes of the exhilarating event. Was it just a dream or had it really happened—this incomparable encounter with the living God of Buddhism, the God of Love!

12

The Tibetan Waiter

Once again I visited our 'Home Joseph 2', which we had opened in 2010 for about fifty Tibetan refugee children. I repeatedly spoke to the Tibetan children about their future careers. For these young and dedicated Tibetans, it is not easy to find a decent job in India, a huge country of almost 1.4 billion people. Though India had become their new home, de facto they were considered foreigners. When you realise that even Indians struggle to find work in their own country, you can imagine how much harder it must be for Tibetan refugee children. Despite their often top-notch education, they are usually stuck with low-paying jobs as tourist guides, jeep drivers or houseboys.

Exceptions are rare, but they do exist. Tenzin (name changed), a young Tibetan, had the rare good fortune to be granted political asylum in Austria at the time of the Tibetan riots during the 2008 Beijing Olympics.

Somehow word had got around among my Tibetan friends that I owned a catering business. So almost every

Tibetan refugee who came to Austria eventually found me and asked for a job. So far, about thirty Tibetans have found a new home in Linz. They are hard-working and well on their way to integration. When they once asked me to help them find a place to live, I was happy to do so and paid a deposit of 4,000 euros, so that they could move into an old house in Linz (unfortunately next to the city's largest brothel). A few years later, when they all had permanent jobs, they paid me back in full.

Tenzin also got a work permit for Austria relatively quickly and, of course, he applied for a job with us. As he spoke almost no German, we first offered him a job in the kitchen. It was not necessary for him to speak our language because he was barely engaging with the customers. After about six months—during which time he also attended German classes—he was promoted to the post of a dishwasher. He soon took the opportunity to work as a waiter and became very popular with the guests.

Tibetan Buddhists in particular have a special way of relating to other people. Their loving, friendly nature is especially appreciated in the service sector. Expertise is of secondary importance, as the well-being of the guest takes precedence. Unfortunately, our Austrian catering experts, once so popular around the world, are increasingly forgetting these important virtues. Tenzin, however, soon became one of the best in his new guild.

He had all the makings of a picture-book career in the catering industry. But nothing came of it. He failed because of the dangers of our European affluence, the temptations of which he was unfortunately unable to resist.

Tibetans tend to grow up in large families. Many fathers and mothers spend weeks at a time with their herds of yaks and sheep in the summer pastures or the fields of the Himalayas.

Their children are usually not brought up by their parents but by the village community. This means that neighbours play a much greater role in family life than relatives, who are rarely at home. Family life in Austria is known to be different.

Soon, Tenzin met a Tibetan woman. He had a healthy son and dutifully went about his daily work in our company. European prosperity brought new luxuries for him. He moved into a nicer and more expensive apartment. The child was taken to the state-funded nursery, in line with the European model of affluence. His wife also began to work so that they could afford the European standards of living. However, it was difficult to reconcile his wife's work with the upbringing of the child. Conflicts on the personal and professional fronts increased.

Things went from bad to worse. Tenzin began to gamble, bet and drink. He was a welcome guest in the many legal gambling dens in the centre of Linz. He soon picked up a reputation as a wealthy and successful man. Many people envied him, but they never talked about how much he gambled—only he knew.

Our office had to frequently come to his rescue by paying him in advance. He kept on gambling with higher stakes. The resulting strain of working on a full-time job and also gambling side by side overwhelmed him. His manager started coming to see me frequently, letting me know each time that he was becoming more of a trouble with each passing day and that 'things couldn't go on like this'. He kept catching him at work 'with customers waiting for their drinks while he was behind the bar betting big money on his mobile phone'.

His wife soon realised what was going on. More and more often, he came home drunk late at night, and it was always 'all the work at the company' that was to blame. There were times he wanted to quit his job, believing in his despair that things would be different in a new job. But I always managed to convince him that nowhere else would he find such an understanding and friendly family as ours. It was true that he earned very well and received a lot of tips.

Unfortunately, he had taken advantage of my absence and had simply not returned to work. Our restaurant manager was again without a waiter. Tenzin's colleagues didn't go along well with him anyway because they had to cover for him all the time. So it was no surprise that they were keeping a very close eye on how we were dealing with his constant misbehaviour.

Almost as a mockery—at a time when I was discussing their future with the young residents of our children's home—I received a text message from my wife in Austria. It had to be urgent because we had agreed to communicate only on important matters.

Tenzin, who had worked so hard and diligently for the past six years, had once again failed to turn up for work. Unexcused absences always result in immediate dismissal. No holiday pay, no salary, nothing. This time my wife went through with it!

I thought about it for a long time until I confirmed my wife's question about the dismissal by text message. A few hours later, I received the following message from Tenzin on Facebook:

> I don't know how to begin. Forgive me for interrupting your holiday. Except I have no choice. I am very ashamed. I am totally exhausted as an addicted gambler and I have lost my concentration and motivation at work and at home! I accept all my mistakes! All of us Tibetans, including me, are always grateful to you for your heartfelt support! I received many chances even though I have brought many of my personal problems to work. But I could not keep up …

this time something worse happened ... my wife was in hospital Wagnerjaureg! And again I couldn't work last Monday! Then I thought it's better to stop working than to always mix private problems with work!

After two days, I went to Mrs Hager in the office and Mrs Hager invited me for a coffee. She understood my problems and gave me a suggestion: I'd lose everything if I stayed at home. Then I apologised to Mrs Hager for my mistake and said I was ready to work for 14 days as notice period. Then she told me to ask the restaurant manager first! After I got a call from Mrs Hager, she told me that the head waiter doesn't want me in the team!

Mrs Hager said that the boss had said a lot about me! However, I have told Mrs Hager many times that she shouldn't do this ... I have a child! I know Mrs Hager's heart is not like that, but the head waiter told me a bad story! I don't care what he told me and I don't understand why he asked me to go back!

I have been working at Josef's since 15 May 2008, and in these five years I have never said a bad word to anyone and I will never say anything even if I am not working there. Maybe he still has text messages from me! I requested him with all my heart! I called him many times and requested him to give me a normal notice, but he didn't hear me. Then I went to Mrs Hager and cried, but she said that Ober had already given the orders! I was completely destroyed and had no help. I then called my friend because he knows me well! [...] Then he told me that Mrs Hager gave me the first go because he said so! All this happened because of my frequent visits to the casino, and I accept my mistakes!

I didn't realise I was getting addicted! I swore in front of my Holy God and my son that I would never play with money again in my life! In the end, my wife accepted me and we hope to have a normal life together.

Dear Mr Hager, I have one last hope, and that is you! I beg you from the bottom of my heart to give me a normal release! Otherwise, my Tibetan colleagues will think that the notice is being cancelled because of ill will and it will be very bad for my son's future! Last time, Mrs Hager told me, 'Tenzin, whether or not you are in Josef, we are always happy.' I will never forget this in my life and I will always be ready for Josef if I am needed! I am signing off with high hopes! Forgive me for the disappointment!

Love, Tenzin

Shortly afterwards I received another message:

Dear Mr Hager, please help me! Today I was laid off without notice from Mrs Hager! Please don't be like this! I'm begging you to grant me a normal termination!

Sitting with my Tibetan friends, I see how the perils of our prosperity are destroying people. This once capable person made it all the way to what seemed to him a perfect world, started a wonderful family, and now he is failing because of a terrible addiction to gambling.

I have been coming to meet my Tibetan friends for years to help spread more knowledge about their culture, but my culture itself is destroying the almost successful, never-ending, painstaking journey of a dear Tibetan friend.

This is what I wrote in my message to my wife:

> Hello Monika,
> It's hard for me to say no. After all, Tenzin has been with us for almost six years. I understand that our restaurant manager is angry, but I don't want to spoil Tenzin's future. Other people beat us up, but not him! He used to be a good waiter, maybe he'll learn!
> Bussi Günter

My wife's reply was as follows:

> I hope you know that your decision will cost us about €5,000, but I know that you and I have already made the transfer!
> Love, Monika

Tenzin sent me a message shortly afterwards:

> Dear Mr Hager, I thank you from the bottom of my heart for your decision and your help! I will never forget it! Thank you again …

I have heard many similar stories over the years in our own company and also while interacting with others.

Later, my very good friend Rigo Tulku sent an email to me asking for help regarding two Tibetan refugee girls. He was planning to fly them to Austria and wanted to know if I would look after them.

I thought about his request for a long time. I discussed the matter with Elisabeth Zimmermann of Save Tibet and also talked to others. After careful consideration, I replied, with some embarrassment, that I thought it would be better for the girls to grow up in their new home in India. 'Many foreigners',

I wrote to him, 'are not up for the dangers of "European social prosperity"', and so I think it would be more sensible if 'they stayed with their families and friends in their exile homeland with modest wages, instead of perishing in the countless dangers of European prosperity.'

Rigo Tulku is not only a good friend but also a sensible man. He understood the deeper meaning of my reply and endeavoured to find a suitable place for the two Tibetan girls in their new home in India.

13

The Opening of the Temple

It was early January, following our hectic gastronomic Christmas season. I had been working about eighteen hours a day for about seven weeks. Christmas parties round the clock. We were thrilled to see that our business was doing so well. But we also desperately needed the turnover to pay off our loans, which had unfortunately increased.

A neighbour who had just moved in was objecting to just about every aspect of the proposed conversion of an underground car park under our beer garden. As a result, the work could not progress for about two years. For us, this meant a loss of business of over 50 per cent. We had enormous financial problems and were forced to lay off twenty-eight people. Of course, everyone has the right to object to such projects. After all, we are lucky enough to live in a democracy. Although our new neighbours didn't win the case in the end, the consequences were disastrous. After our successful appeal, we were able to resume work. But we were left with a huge debt. It was an economic disaster. I never saw the neighbour again—she had simply moved away in anger at losing the case. But once again I'd had enough. I was fed up with the daily grind and the people who wanted to stop everything. So I planned a well-deserved relaxing holiday in Phuket for my wife and myself.

Having not had a chance to open my many Christmas cards during the stressful Christmas period, I did so during the rather quiet New Year period. Among them was a mail from my Buddhist friend Rigo Tulku Rinpoche from the Himalayas. I recognised this at first glance because he used only handmade paper. I had assumed that Rigo Tulku's letter was a Christmas card, but the reason for his letter was quite different. The envelope contained the official invitation to the opening ceremony of his new three-storey temple in the Himalayas. What an honour! There was no way I could refuse and, honestly, I didn't want to.

So, the first thing I had to do was explain to my wife that the luxury holiday I had planned in Phuket was not going to work out. It was easier than I thought. My wife didn't want to stand in the way of my great joy of being able to attend this event. The opening date of the monastery was 1 April 2012—but not an April Fool's joke. So, I began to plan my trip and booked a flight to Delhi.

For those unfamiliar with India, travelling to the Himalayas can be an odyssey. But it wasn't my first trip. With the right flight connections and the right local jeep drivers, it is possible to get from Europe to this special place in just twenty-four hours.

Luckily, my plan worked once again. I arrived in Tso Pema a few days before the opening. My first stop was going to be a visit to my friend Rigo Tulku Rinpoche. He had seen me coming from a distance. He greeted me with a smile and wanted to know if I had had a good journey. He informed me that the numerous high-profile guests and the last-minute arrangements for the temple's inauguration ceremony left him with little time for me. However, he told me to contact him at any time if I needed anything. I could use the monk's hermitage that had been prepared for me for as long as I wanted. The permanent occupant of this small room, a young monk, like so many others, had been moved to a large, shared dormitory for the days leading to the ceremony. The small, newly built monks' huts were reserved for the guests of honour at the opening ceremony and, very kindly, for me. I shared this honour with important local politicians and senior lamas who had travelled from far and wide.

The only furnishings were a tiny wardrobe, a wooden chair and a small bed. There was also an extra room for cooking and a toilet—unfortunately without a water supply. The facilities were very modest. No flat screen, no hi-fi system with speakers, no telephone. No Internet or other luxuries adorned this simple but beautiful room overlooking the small Indian town of Rewalsar.

Early in the morning, child monks would quietly place a bucket of cold water in front of my hermitage to wash myself. I had to use it very sparingly, for water was always scarce.

I stayed in this beautiful place for a few days before the opening. During that time, I helped the monks clean the premises of the temple. There was a lot of work to do. Soon, the new tables and benches were delivered for the opening ceremony. Twisting energy-saving bulbs into the lampshades on a high scaffolding is a real feat at dizzying heights. But in the end—and I won't say any more about this—it was quite funny seeing the monks in their skirts doing their gymnastics.

Of course, I took the opportunity to take many wonderful and unique photos of the hustle and bustle in this newly built, unique temple.

I also met a Buddhist millionaire from Singapore. He had donated towards most of the expenses of the temple and had arrived with his financial assistant and secretary. Rigo Tulku Rinpoche had known him for a long time. I got the opportunity to have breakfast with the three of them almost every day on the terrace of the monastery. Fortunately, as in our latitudes in the Catholic world, there are always generous people who help finance such magnificent temples and thus support the continuity of Buddhist culture.

I have been observing the construction of this magnificent three-storey structure called the Nyingmapa Palyul Choekhorling Buddhist Temple in Tso Pema for many years. It has always been a special place, perched above a sacred lake hidden by the Himalayas. It is said that Padmasambhava (Guru Rinpoche), the great Buddhist saint and reformer, meditated at the site for a long time in a cave back in the eighth century.

Rigo Tulku Rinpoche repeatedly invited me to his monastery in Bir during my visits. Together, we often undertook the three-hour journey to the temple site in Rewalsar to check on the progress of the work. About thirty hard-working migrant workers from Bhutan, probably the last country where Tibetan Buddhism is still practised as a true state religion, were busy decorating the temple ceilings, modelling the statues and painting the walls of the new structure. I was lucky to be the only European to be able to follow and observe the construction of one of the most beautiful Tibetan temples in the Himalayas—that too for more than five years.

Back at his huge monastery in Bir, Rigo showed me the huge thangkas he had skilfully made for the new temple in Bhutan—

which now adorned the new temple—along with hundreds of small gilded Buddhas. They were painstakingly handcrafted, sculpted, inscribed with mantras and intricately gilded.

The artworks were brought together in the newly built temple at Tso Pema after years of hard work and finally found their rightful place in the magnificent Tibetan temple, one of its kind in India! The main hall on the ground floor was dominated by a huge, shimmering gilded statue of Guru Rinpoche. The reincarnation of Buddha himself, the statue towers mightily over the heads of his enemies, all impaled on a spear. It was surrounded by statues of eight Bodhisattvas.

To put it bluntly, these so-called guardian gods could be compared to our guardian angels. To the right and left of the giant statue were two huge thangkas. In the foreground, however, was a mighty, ornately decorated throne. His Holiness the Dalai Lama was to arrive to perform the grand opening ceremony.

Thousands of Buddhist pilgrims had gathered. They were all there to witness the imminent inauguration by the Dalai Lama. As the Dalai Lama travels around the world for around 240 days a year, Tibetans take every opportunity to be close to their living god.

Tibetans had travelled from the farthest mountains and valleys of the Himalayas to witness this unique event. Chanting mantras, they travelled clockwise around the sacred mystical lake of Tso Pema on their ancient prayer wheels.

It is said that Padmasambhava was burnt on a huge funeral pyre by the powerful king of the nearby town of Mandi and father of the beloved princess Mandarava. However, after his own cremation, Padmasambhava transformed the glowing pyre into a magnificent lake, now known as Tso Pema. From its centre grew a huge and beautiful lotus flower from which he himself, Padmasambhava, was reborn—hence getting the nickname 'the lotus-born'.

The area, still relatively undiscovered by tourists, has been one of the great holy pilgrimage sites for Buddhists ever since. For my friend Rigo Tulku, this was certainly one of the reasons behind choosing the beautiful site for his magnificent temple.

Many pilgrims slept in cloth tents on the edge of the sacred lake. Campfires burned in old oil barrels; mothers breastfed their babies; and simple makeshift Tibetan eateries served yak butter tea and Tibetan dumplings.

I compared the arrangements to the city fairs in my hometown of Linz. There was a stark difference—there was no clamour from the tourist. There was no noise, no honking and no drunken shouting. Peacefully, they walked clockwise around the holy lake, wearing their colourful festive dresses, murmuring their mantras incessantly. One hundred and eight laps around the holy Mount Kailash in distant Tibet gives a Buddhist the ubiquitous desire to come closer to nirvana—similar to our longing for the kingdom of heaven. For the pilgrims gathered, it was the holy lake that I had to give up after only four laps due to lack of stamina.

A huge tent was erected next to the monastery. Hundreds of helpers and guests were being catered for. Tibetan women were busy chopping vegetables while the monks were preparing food in big pots. As a friendly and welcoming gesture, I was allowed to visit and photograph everything without a word of criticism. In fact, I was repeatedly invited to taste the food. There was no hustle and bustle about the upcoming event. The monks were completely relaxed as they went about their last tasks before the grand opening. Two monks were busy setting up butter lamps in brass bowls. There must have been about 500 of them. A small wick was pressed into each lamp, which was then filled with melted yak fat and soon hundreds of lights were flickering on the altar of the Great Buddha. The Tibetan pilgrims were already starting to circle the temple, though we were still cleaning the forecourt together.

As always, I had a pipe, plenty of tobacco and a box of good cigars in my luggage. For me, there was nothing better than being able to enjoy them in complete peace and quiet in a particularly romantic place. Getting into the mysterious and natural flow of things has always been a very conscious form of meditation for me. Many of my chapters in this book were written in such inspiring moments.

Soon it was time for the opening. People had lined up patiently along the narrow access road to the monastery. Some monks were still busy drawing huge cultic ornaments on the tarmac road, painted in white without using any tools or grids and yet the final results showed an unprecedented perfect symmetry.

Access to the temple grounds was cordoned off. Only a select few were allowed in. For the life of me, I couldn't recognise any white-skinned foreigners. I was the only European there—and probably the guest who had travelled from afar. What a special honour to be invited!

The whole monastery was filled with smoke. Right in front of my hermitage, huge quantities of dry brushwood had been set alight to announce the arrival of His Holiness. An endless red carpet had been laid from the car parking spot to the many steps of the temple on the hill. All the monks had put on their festive costumes, wearing huge yellow caps as they stood in a line along the carpet.

Several jeeps with flashing blue lights could be seen approaching the temple. Police officers armed with sub-machine guns got out and secured the access road. Behind them, His

Holiness arrived in a dark green shiny jeep. The monks began blowing their endlessly long Tibetan brass alphorns. A second group struck huge brass cymbals with an unheard and unseen intensity. Another group blew their snow-white, ornately decorated conch-shell horns, producing shrill and endlessly sustained tones. No loudspeakers or electronic amplifiers could support such impressive sounds. These were the same sounds that have been produced using home-made instruments made of bone, wood or metal since time immemorial. Then, as now, they were used to ward off evil spirits and also help people know whether there were any honoured guests inside the temple. It all made for an eerie, yet beautiful and mysterious music, one that filled the whole valley and could even be heard in the smallest of corners. I felt a shiver run down my spine. I could not and did not want to hide my deep emotions and cried silently to myself. I was witnessing a ceremony that was centuries, perhaps millennia old—and one that only a few white people had ever witnessed.

The crowd along the road bowed deeply and people raised their white khatas as a sign of their joy. The long-awaited leader of all Tibetans in the world had arrived.

The Dalai Lama got out of the car outside my monastic hermitage. Dozens of monks stood ready to escort him into the temple guest house, protected by a huge orange canopy.

I took hundreds of photographs as if I were a possessed man. Feeling extremely tense and excited, there was a question lurking in my head: 'What if the photos don't come out right? I had to bring these impressive pictures home in one piece, still tainted by my Western ego, to show everyone what I had experienced. I hastily changed the lens and continued to take countless pictures of His Holiness's arrival and the colourful procession of monks following him.

When the group around the Dalai Lama suddenly disappeared into the small, newly built structure, I couldn't resist following them—this was the best chance I'd have to get some unique pictures. I also wanted to get to the temple as quickly as possible to be ready when His Holiness began the opening ceremony. But I hadn't reckoned with the security check that had been set up in the meantime. One of His Holiness's armed escorts firmly refused to allow me entry. 'This far and no further' was the clear signal, although I obviously could understand him. This took me completely by surprise. After all, I was one of the guests of Rigo Tulku Rinpoche, the builder of this magnificent temple. The security guard told me that I could only enter without a camera. Only a selected photographer was allowed to attend the ceremony and I was not that person. Anger and disappointment washed over me. Why had I dragged two cameras, all my photographic equipment with telephoto lenses and tripods up there? I had been waiting for this moment for days! Not to have captured this rare event would have been a huge disappointment. But what could one do about the security guard who was stubbornly following orders. He was, after all, just doing his job.

When Rigo Tulku's brother happened to be passing by, we tried a trick together. We decided to put a sticker from one of Austria's biggest dailies to the huge interchangeable lens of one of my cameras. I had bought it from my friend Christian, who was a press photographer there. I still had an old Austrian newspaper in my room. So I went down to the hermitage and got the paper. Armed with it, I tried to tell the grim security guard in my poor English: 'I come from far away, from Austria, and I work as a journalist for this newspaper,' pointing demonstratively at the sticker and the newspaper's logo to support my bad English. And it worked. He looked at me closely and asked if I had two passport photographs. Of course I did. So I went back down to the hermitage, grabbed two passport photographs, got my passport and returned to the spot. The back and forth was almost like a marathon, especially in the scorching heat, but the final photographs I could eventually manage to click were worth it! I had to wait for about half an hour before I saw Rigo Tulku's brother returning, smiling, holding a Tibetan press card wrapped tightly in plastic. Now I finally had the long-awaited permission to photograph the opening ceremony in the temple—alongside the only 'chosen' photographer present. What stress, what trepidation, but what joy!

It was about two o'clock in the afternoon. The forecourt of the temple was crowded with guests of honour. They were all waiting anxiously. I managed to find a slightly elevated spot at the entrance to the temple from where I had a good view of everything.

The Dalai Lama arrived. He waved to us with a benevolent smile. Then the whole entourage, including the guests of honour, circled the magnificent three-storey building in a clockwise direction before finally stopping inside the temple, around a huge golden throne.

From then on, I tried to capture every little moment of the ceremony that followed. I kept changing my position, using the three huge access doors to get the best lighting. Fortunately, the invited guests of honour were happy to make room for me.

The Dalai Lama mounted the huge golden throne. Standing slightly behind him, reserved and somewhat stooped, was his secretary and nephew, Tenzin Taklha, who accompanies him on his travels around the world, always in the service of His Holiness. Next to him was the unfortunately indispensable head of the bodyguard. I had also known him for a long time. I first met him in 2005 at Melk Abbey, during my first audience with the Dalai Lama. If I wasn't mistaken, His Holiness's bodyguard, who usually looks sombre and tense, gave me a smile and a wink.

At the entrance gates facing the three cardinal points, the guests of honour were still streaming into the now overcrowded temple and taking their seats on the benches I had helped set up.

This time, I positioned myself next to my cameraman at the central entrance gate, directly opposite His Holiness inside the temple. Another tall bodyguard checked my 'press pass' again. I grinned proudly with an 'I'm allowed in' look on my face, and as if everyone had been waiting for me, the ceremony began.

First there were endless mantras and deep chants from the monks. Then the Dalai Lama read from prayer cards printed in Tibetan script, swaying from side to side to the rhythm of the prayer in his characteristic way. This was followed by speeches from my friend Rigo Tulku Rinpoche, high Tibetan dignitaries, Indian government officials and old lamas. Of course, the only language spoken was Tibetan, so I didn't understand a word. But it didn't matter. It wasn't just me who seemed to be enchanted by the magical atmosphere, it seemed to hypnotise everyone in the room. Shy at first, but then a little braver, I went to the other two gates during the ceremony. I carefully climbed over the many monks sitting on the benches and on the floor and took great photographs—getting ever braver as I got closer to His Holiness. I often had the impression that the Dalai Lama was smiling at me. I was sure he had recognised my face. The Dalai Lama was to present certificates to about thirty aspiring lamas who had completed their studies. The local photographer was feeling a bit overwhelmed. Somehow, he could not manage to get a picture of everyone together with His Holiness, as everyone wanted a souvenir photo with His Holiness. He looked at me, seeking help. There it was, the opportunity of a lifetime. So I went up to His Holiness with my camera. Each time, I would gently push one of the aspiring lamas next to His Holiness, ask briefly with the words 'Please smile, His Holiness' and take a photograph. The Dalai Lama and the honoured guests smiled at me about thirty times! For a short time, I was the Master of Ceremonies during this unique initiation. How unbelievably beautiful!

A month later, at another private audience in Salzburg, the Dalai Lama pointed to me in the crowd and said: 'I remember you, sir.'

'Yes, Your Holiness,' I replied, 'it was in Tso Pema at the opening of my friend Rigo Tulku Rinpoche's wonderful temple. I was invited there as a guest.'

He nodded and then laughed. He had indeed memorised my face from among the many guests and admirers who were introduced to him every day.

About fifty monks had lined up in the forecourt of the temple, carrying precious gifts. Finely chiselled silver cups, ornate candlesticks, sumptuous robes, finely woven Tibetan rugs, gilded Buddha statues—all treasures of unimaginable value. These were to be presented to the Dalai Lama as gifts. I didn't quite understand how it could be reconciled with the Buddhist vow of modesty. But things turned out differently than my capitalistically pre-programmed brain had imagined it would.

Though all the precious gifts were offered to the Dalai Lama, he rejected them with a clear wave of his hand, apparently in accordance with an ancient ritual. The magnificent objects were thus kept as the property of the monastery and disappeared into the depths of the caves beneath the temple building, stored away for future generations and worse times.

The opening ceremony slowly drew to a close. I had used just about every lens and camera I had brought with me, hoping the photographs would turn out great. I knew they would be rare testimony to a very special event. The many dignitaries came in as part of His Holiness's entourage to the forecourt of the temple, which looked mystical in the setting sun, and greeted the many people present once again. The Dalai Lama spoke to some of them, shook hands and waved to those behind him with a friendly smile. After that, he disappeared into the small house above my hermitage, where he spent the night.

I sat for a long time under the evening sun in the temple forecourt, forgetting about dinner, but enthusiastically going through the many photographs on my camera. What a day, what an experience! I kept looking in the direction of His Holiness's lighted room. Then it was dark—even the King of God gets tired and needs to sleep. Would he dream as beautifully as I did?

He left early in the morning, accompanied by his secretaries and security guards. I had slept through everything. But I was still proud to be the only European to have witnessed such an extraordinary and rare experience.

Postscript: Back at home, I sent Rigo Tulku a USB stick with the photographs of the lamas by post. Unfortunately, he couldn't do anything with it due to the absence of hardware. A year later, I gave him a photo book with the best clicks of the opening of his temple and another stick with the photographs of the opening, including, of course, the enthronement photos of the lamas with their living God-King.

My photographs are now available for sale as postcards and giant posters, reprinted thousands of times in the markets of the Rewalsar region. And yes, they still adorn the monasteries of the venerable lamas.

14

Inside the Cave of Padmasambhava

In our packed jeep, we headed downstream towards Mandi*, which is located at the entrance to the legendary Kullu Valley. All in all, the journey took about three hours.

Our actual destination was the mountain village of Rewalsar (Tibetan: Tso Pema), along with the mysterious Tso Pema (Mother Lake), which is just a few kilometres from Mandi. Many stories surround this sacred site, which is important to Buddhists, Hindus and Sikhs. Even today, hundreds of monks live in the mountains around Rewalsar, usually for years at a stretch in absolute solitude, away from the public eye.

Rigo Tulku Rinpoche had invited me to visit the mysterious cave of the great Buddhist reformer Padmasambhava. My friend Rigo Tulku is the head lama of the Buddhist Nyingmapa lineage.

I was able to see the huge temple complex, which sat majestically on a hill above the holy lake. The golden roofs of the unique building was visible from afar. The romantic mountain lake in front of it was teeming with sacred fish, fed by the many pilgrims walking around it. On the opposite side of the lake, a huge statue of Guru Padmasambhava could be seen. The 50-metre-tall figure seemed to be smiling at each visitor. For me, it was a kind of 'eternal smile', the magic of which cannot be described in words.

The different colour schemes of the temple buildings represented different faiths. Not far from the Rigo Tulku's temple was another huge temple complex, almost snow-like in colour. It was a holy place of worship for Sikh priests and their followers. Nowhere else have I seen so many different religions practising their culture and beliefs in such harmony. This can only work with respect and mutual tolerance—only up in the Himalayas.

In this context, I remember an annoying media frenzy in my hometown of Linz. It was triggered by the construction of a small Buddhist stupa, comparable to a Catholic chapel. There was a lot of excitement, especially among the neighbours. Partly supported by the press, they tried to stop the project. It was suspected that a 'dangerous sect' would set up shop there. A quick search at Google or Wikipedia would have prevented many a senseless smear campaign.

Padmasambhava, who brought Buddhism to Tibet from India around AD 800, is said to have meditated in a nearby cave in Rewalsar for several years. Rigo Tulku had already shown me the cave, which was hidden high up in the mountains, from a distance. One couldn't miss the entrance, decorated with countless prayer flags. The rustling of the colourful cloth, printed with mantras, created a strange background noise which was mystically amplified by the echo of the sheer cliffs on the opposite side.

As I climbed, I closed my eyes and could visualise the mantras printed on the prayer flags floating down the valley like thousands of swallows. If you allow yourself to imagine, the surroundings become a special mystical place, a place that invites you to dream. My friend seemed to have already lost himself in it. At the opening of the cave, he had begun to murmur ancient Tibetan mantras in a mysterious language that I couldn't identify. As if in a trance, he moved barefoot into the cave carved into the rock.

The visit to the depths of the mountain was mystical and mysterious. The cave was wet and humid, lit by an enormous number of yak butter candles flickering in the dim light. A gilded statue of Buddha Padmasambhava shone impressively in the shimmering candlelight. Sometimes, for just a few minutes, when the midday sun was very high, its rays would shine through the narrow open cracks above the statue on to the ever-smiling face. Then—and only for that short time—the Buddha would shine and glow as if the power of his aura would bring down the entire mountain.

In a side cave, I saw a slightly smaller statue, probably a representation of his wife, the Indian princess Mandarava. Legend has it that Padmasambhava got married in the Himalayas against the will of the king of Mandi.

Hundreds of white kathas hung on the walls as small gifts from pilgrims. Donation bowls filled with banknotes stood in front of the altar where Rinpoche had knelt. Despite the damp, dirty floor, he threw himself on the ground in front of the shining golden statue and paid his respects to the most powerful of all Buddhas.

I stood close to my friend but felt uncomfortable. I wanted to be an invisible spectator and was ashamed of my insecurity. Rigo Tulku was now completely in trance and his mantras grew louder and louder as the golden Padmasambhava looked down on his humble son with a benevolent smile.

Like him, Rigo Tulku himself is a famous reincarnation, an ever-reborn Buddhist manifestation on the endless path to heavenly nirvana. Rigo Tulku finished his mantra and slowly returned to reality. He stood up and bowed deeply to the Buddha once more. Then he smiled at me and gestured that our visit was over.

We sat together for a long time on the bench in front of the cave, gazing out into the wide valley in silence, as the great Buddha Padmasambhava must have done thousands of years ago, dreaming of his beloved.

It became one of my favourite places up there in the Himalayas. On each of my many visits, I walked among the countless forests of Tibetan prayer flags fluttering in the mountain breeze. Pilgrims have tied tens of thousands of these seemingly ghostly flags to the few trees and rocks here, so that the wind can carry the prayers written on the cloth out into the wide world. The mantras are meant to bring happiness and contentment to the people out there—and it is hoped that this will lead to rebirth in the next, hopefully better and happier life.

Every good Buddhist lives a life that is entirely focused on avoiding the three big sins of greed, avarice and anger, leading a virtuous life and practising charity in order to be reborn.

Such a principle is similar to the ones found in Christianity, Hinduism and Islam. During its history and reforms, each religion has experienced positive and, unfortunately, negative times. Buddhism has been no exception. But the true, ultimate goal of almost all religions can be found in charity, mindfulness, peace and personal happiness.

Immediately after our visit to the cave, we took a jeep back to the small town of Bir, the starting point of our journey. The journey began with a descent through the little hamlet of Mandi, located at the mouth of the Kullu Valley, and ended with an ascent through the Kangra Valley, passing by an endless stretch of tea terraces.

If there is one area in India where Tibetans cherish their traditions and try to live by them, it is here. I often refer to the region as the 'second little Tibet', although the vast tea plantations and unexpected vegetation do not necessarily reflect the more barren high valley of Tibet. The fact is that many Tibetan families have settled in the area, following and practising their culture more intensively than anywhere else in the world. Four huge Tibetan monasteries, with hundreds of monks, have settled in the region and continue their millennia-old way of life. Buddhist child monks study their religion and continue with their education in the mysterious world of Buddhism. Monasteries, with up to 2,000 monks, testify to the influx in the peaceful, beautiful region at the foot of the Himalayas.

But tourism is likely to leave its mark in Bir too. I am thinking of the shortage of young Catholic priests in our latitudes. As is so often the case, it is prosperity and a lack of interest in compassion. No wonder we are left with few successors to Christian priests and monks.

Vast tea plantations dominate the countryside around Bir, giving it a lovely atmosphere. The village itself lies at an altitude of around 2,000 metres. Temperatures rarely go below the freezing point and rarely rise above 35 degrees in summer. It is a climatically unique place, as has been evident from the influx of prominent figures from local politics and religion. Many have set up their summer homes in the area. Respected Buddhist institutes have also set up shop, attracting knowledge-hungry Buddhist tourists from all over the world.

Three huge SOS Children's Villages (TCV Suja, TCV Chauntra and TCV Gopalpur) for around 5,000 Tibetan refugee children have been built here with the help of generous sponsors. In 2006, I was able to celebrate the impressive opening of my first 'Home Josef' in the Indian village of Suja, right next to Bir, in the presence of around 3,000 guests. It marked the beginning of a special relationship between the Tibetan people and me.

I would like to tell you a funny story that happened shortly before the opening of my 'Home Josef 1'.

A few days before the opening ceremony, I sent an email to the SOS Children's Village asking them to organise a lunch for the students, participants and my guests, also including, if possible, some Tibetan folk dance performances.

I was to be accompanied by a camera crew from an Austrian TV station, and of course they wanted some good footage.

Shortly before I left, I contacted them to make sure everything was organised and to find out how many guests would actually be coming. When I got the answer, I literally froze on the phone. Lobsang, the organiser of the opening ceremony, said that there would be about 2,500 children, and with the teachers, guests of honour and monks coming, there would be another 500. So there would be a total of about 3,000 guests!

Of course, I didn't expect so many people, but I went ahead with it anyway. I was happy to pay the almost ridiculously small amount of 50 cents per person for lunch out of my own pocket. It was worth it. Never before in my catering career had I seen such happy people, myself included.

The opening ceremony took place at noon. It was a very hot day. A fellow traveller from Austria wanted to help Rinpoche Rigo Tulku Rinpoche, who was sitting next to me. He asked me to give him a small hand fan to cool him down. Rigo Tulku accepted it gratefully at first. Then he took a quick look at it and gave it back with a smile saying, 'No, thanks—it is made in China.'

Rigo Tulku, who ran a huge Buddhist monastery in the village with around 600 monks, inaugurated our first orphanage. Since then, we have had a very deep bond. He even visited me in Austria with his brother and stayed at my house for several days in the beautiful Mühlviertel region.

In the evening, I was invited to Rigo Tulku's house. Although I kept wondering whether I could hug and embrace him, I decided to bow with folded hands, as the monks did. The Tulku (reborn) took my hand and led me to the first floor of his monastery, to his favourite place, which he had set up in front of a small window. From there, he could easily see everything that was going on in his huge monastery. We looked at each other for a long time in silence, for Rigo's command of English was as poor as mine.

In his audience room, there were many photographs hanging on the wall next to the huge armchair. One was of German Tibet activist Wegner. Now almost ninety years old, she was said to have organised around a thousand sponsorships for Tibetan refugee children. She was now living in Munich, Rigo told me proudly, and was an old acquaintance of his. I didn't know at the time that we would be visiting her together about a year later. Next to it was a photograph of my wife Monika and me—a sign of the mutual esteem he and I shared.

I sat on my balcony for a long time that night, puffing on the pipe I had brought with me. I thought about our much-vaunted European prosperity. The constant struggle for prosperity had brought me here, where I could finally find the peace I had been seeking for so long.

15

At Home in Dharamshala

Two small, dirty and substandard roads mark the centre of McLeodganj, a suburb about 5 kilometres above Dharamshala in Kangra district. It is also known as 'Little Lhasa' or 'Dhasa' (a shortened form of Dharamshala used mainly by Tibetans). One of these narrow streets leads downhill to the Dalai Lama Temple. Richard Gere, film star and long-time friend of the Dalai Lama, generously had it resurfaced and tarred to give the many pilgrims a better route to the monastery temple. Because of his commitment to the Tibetan people, even this world-famous film star has long been banned from entering China. Like a true Buddhist, Richard Gere has often commented that he considers it a great honour to accept this ban for his support to the Tibetans.

I was lucky that the Dalai Lama was in the vicinity. It was a rare opportunity because he spends about 70 per cent of the year travelling. So it's difficult to meet him. Of course, I'm not the only one who wanted to see him. With the school holidays just beginning in parts of India, the streets of McLeodganj were flooded with Buddhist pilgrims. Thousands of his followers also made the journey to attend the Dalai Lama's four-day teaching. Many of them arrived in packed jeeps, like the ones I came across in Bir, a mountain village about 70 kilometres from Dharamshala. They were Tibetans from faraway Spiti, close to the Chinese border. It is only now that I can easily recognise them by their sumptuous Tibetan dress and intricately braided hair. They were mostly women with their children, who travelled all the way to see their living god in Dharamshala. At the wheel were men whose wrinkled facial skin had turned a dark yellow-brown with decades of working under the sun.

I also met many European solo travellers, and Israelis taking advantage of a cheap holiday from military service. I met philosophers and journalists, as well as brave women travelling alone to train at the many yoga and reiki schools. They all had one thing in common—they wanted to seize the opportunity to see the Dalai Lama in person once in their lives.

Photos of Richard Gere, Goldie Hawn, Madonna, Antonio Banderas, Desmond Tutu and countless other friends of the Dalai Lama are plastered on the walls of monasteries and homes, which bear witness to their visits up there. It often feels as if I've seen the odd passers-by in a blockbuster film.

It's remarkable how quickly visitors adapt to the local way of dressing. I myself swapped my thick, fashionable anorak for a finely woven Tibetan yak-hair blanket early on. It has been with me on my travels ever since. It cools and warms at the same time, and is much lighter and more comfortable to wear than our high-tech winter gear. As is so often the case, what advertisements tell us is not the truth. On my pilgrimage, the usual competition from fashion labels, branded mobile phones and other status symbols I'm used to at home faded relatively quickly. The real admiration belongs to the Buddhist pilgrims. They all come from the mountains of the nearby Himalayas, where they live in their village communities. None of them need television or the Internet. Instead, they undertake weeks of arduous travel to meet the 'Kundun' (a Tibetan word meaning "the Presence"), the 'ocean of wisdom', the living god of the Buddhists, the Dalai Lama, once again in their lives. This is the only place where you can experience and feel the influence that the Dalai Lama and the many spiritual dignitaries have on the followers of this culture and on every newcomer.

Love and charity are the pillars of the Buddhist philosophy of life, along with tolerance and self-confidence. This is my idea of paradise. If there is an afterlife, the path to it might give me a similar feeling. Once again, I was in my dream world—the pilgrim from Europe had arrived! *The Tibetan Book of the Dead* speaks of life after death, rebirth in another life, the eternal cycle of dharma and the Buddhist wheel of life. It all depends on how you have organised your present life! How similar most of the great religions are.

But my Western life as an innkeeper is quite the opposite. It is characterised by a hectic pace, stress and going full throttle in order to be a contributing and successful citizen of society. It is also marked by the philosophy of never giving up, always wanting to win, only going forward until ... until nothing else works! My longing for the apparent paradise in the intermediate world of *The Tibetan Book of the Dead* is often greater than the strength to carry on. More and more often it has been my reason to return to the Himalayas.

My visits to my Tibetan friends have increased steadily in recent years. Is it my past that keeps on calling me? These memories keep coming back to me—there is this strange feeling as if I had been part of the mysterious culture in a much earlier time. The old Tibetan friends, the many aged monks, the wailing songs of the women and children, the deep chanting of the lamas—I must have experienced all of that before, maybe a long, long time ago, in a truly different life. And once again I ask myself the crucial question: Does reincarnation exist and was I one of them?

Only those who have been allowed to experience these realisations and only those who have recognised the hamster wheel in which we live here in the West know what to say about the superficiality of our crazy environment. Only those who have had the opportunity to experience and appreciate the kindness, cultural richness and respect of the Tibetan people in the Himalayas will understand what I mean. There, everyone has the opportunity to present their true personality, reduced to their personal knowledge, the echo of their origins. And that becomes the chance to make an honest first impression. Everything else is up to you—your actions, your behaviour, your future, your next life.

Many visitors grow beards. Long hair is worn loose, and the women wear colourful scarves wrapped around their hair, like veils. A group of monks, some of whom have travelled from monasteries far away in the mountains of Bhutan—often equipped with mobile phones—sit over a cup of butter tea. But I have also met many a European nun, their hair shorn into a monk-like bald head—all signs of them visibly leaving behind their hectic European home. Rucksacks are stowed away, bags of essentials carefully guarded. There are also groups of yogis in their orange robes, with long beards, carrying only the most essential utensils wrapped in a cloth.

On the busy streets, unkempt women, hailing from distant Bihar, could be seen begging with babies in their arms—perfectly organised groups of beggars, just like the eastern

European begging mafia on our European luxury shopping streets.

But my favourite spot was on the terrace of the Tibetan café, Kunga Guest House, which was owned by Nick. To me, it seemed that people from all cultures of the world met and mingled there, peacefully and always in good spirits. At first, I was annoyed by the poor WiFi access, but now I use the time to write down my impressions of travelling there, without Facebook and email getting in the way. Nick has three WiFi accounts with very original passwords: 'ChocolateCake', 'FreeTibet' and 'Olivepizza'.

My cigars were nowhere to be found. I needed a pipe and some tobacco. Luckily, Nick had prepared for this too. First, he served me a cold Kingfisher beer—well disguised in a teacup, of course. Nick didn't have a liquor licence for his café. Hemingway must have had a similar experience. Did he realise that his travel stories would be followed by hordes of tourists?

For me, no trip to Asia could be complete without a Singapore Sling at the legendary Raffles Hotel in Singapore. I love the awe-inspiring colonial halls of the Oriental Mandarin Hotel in Bangkok. Everything is exactly as Hemingway so aptly described it. Many of his books have also lured and seduced me into visiting true luxury resorts. But here I love the simplicity, away from the hustle and bustle of Europe and my catering factory.

I never travel to the region without my two favourite books. One is *In the Footsteps of Buddha* written by Marc De Smedt—not Peter van Ham—who was one of the first to beautifully describe his journey from Shimla to the ancient Tibetan monasteries in Spiti in the mysterious Misty Valley and up to Ladakh in the book. Fortunately, I was probably the first Austrian to follow his tour, with the same jeep agency in

Shimla. Mohit Sharma, the owner, has been a dear friend of mine for years.

The second indispensable book on my travels is Heinrich Harrer's *Seven Years in Tibet*. I am always fascinated by his travel experiences. His name is still mentioned with reverence in northern India and every Tibetan knows that this great Austrian traveller was once the teacher of the Dalai Lama. Harrer did much to bring the fate of the Tibetans to the attention of the world. I have been trying to follow in his footsteps for more than twenty years now.

I remember that Harrer was a guest in my gourmet restaurant in Linz on several occasions in the 1980s. I got the opportunity to cook for him and offer him our hospitality. Oh, if only I had realised back then what an important personality had come as a guest in my restaurant!

Today, when I walk through McLeodganj, Tibetan friends wave to me with smiles. Guests who keep coming back are remembered. Rarely have I experienced a place where people are so loving and welcoming! Once, when I left my passport in an Indian office during the extremely tedious and bureaucratic process of trying to get a local mobile phone, it was returned to me personally the next day, with a friendly smile, as if it were the most natural thing in the world to do.

'The people in the mountains are honest and very hospitable, just like the Tibetans and the Austrians,' His Holiness had said with his typical grin.

16

'Amala': The Mother of Tibet

Today, the word 'happiness' has taken on a new meaning for me! At the check-in desk of Kangra Airport, near Dharamshala, I met an elderly woman, who was walking gracefully, wearing a Tibetan dress. We looked at each other as we passed. I could sense the same thought running through both of our minds: 'Do we know each other?'

She gave me a peaceful Tibetan smile and I greeted her warmly in return and bowed briefly. My hands were so full of bags and gifts that I couldn't bring them together to do a proper Tibetan greeting. I suddenly realised who was standing there! It was none other than Amala Jetsun Pema, respectfully known as 'Amala', the mother of all Tibetan refugee children and the sister of His Holiness.

It was as if she could read my mind, for she suddenly spoke to me: 'Hello, we know each other! I have seen you many times in the office of Mr Tsewang Jeshe, my successor as president of the Tibetan SOS Children's Villages in McLeodganj. You built the two orphanages in Dharamshala and the Old People's Home for the hundred mountain nomads in Ladakh. How wonderful to meet you here! May I take this opportunity to thank you most sincerely for your generosity and charity towards our people.'

Completely surprised, I bowed to her again in gratitude for this great compliment, this time very deeply and reverently. I could hardly believe it—the sister of the Dalai Lama was actually standing in front of me, in the middle of the Himalayas!

The story of Heinrich Harrer's *Seven Years in Tibet* with Brad Pitt, in which she played herself and which has been made into a film many times over, ran through my mind as I stared at this wonderful, graceful, almost eighty-year-old Tibetan woman. No one at home will believe me. She really is a celebrity. I was very proud of the fact that she recognised me and took the time to talk to me. Thank you, Amala!

Providence continued to smile on me. I was to meet her again just a few weeks later at a Tibetan festival in Hüttenberg, Carinthia. This time, Amala had more time and was more talkative. I will never forget her detailed stories about Harrer during his time as the Dalai Lama's teacher, and also the little, perhaps completely unknown, memory she shared with me. Whenever she visited her brother in the Potala Palace, as a little girl, she was allowed to sit on Harrer's shoulders and play with his blond hair. What a beautiful memory to have!

Amala Jetsun Pema was born in Lhasa shortly after the Dalai Lama's enthronement. She went to India at the tender age of ten and studied first at St Joseph's Monastery in Kalimpong and later at Loreto Monastery. She then moved to Switzerland and from there to England to further her education.

At the request of her elder brother, she became the president of the Tibetan Children's Villages, a position she held for forty-two years, until she retired. She was instrumental in building the huge organisation of TCVs in Dharamshala and in other places in India. The project she founded today includes thirty-five children's villages, and also schools and homes for the elderly. The future of more than 15,000 Tibetan children and young people is in her hands. In 1990, she became the first Tibetan woman minister. This woman has borne all the suffering of her people. She has witnessed their exodus, the exodus of a people who carry within them one of the most precious cultures and last legacies of humanity, the spiritual sciences of Buddhism as a religion. We in distant Europe have no idea about how much the joint projects of the Austrian founder of the SOS Children's Villages, Hermann Gmeiner, and Amala helped to preserve and protect their culture after the exodus of their people.

After Harrer, Gmeiner was the second well-known Austrian to help many Tibetans after their escape. In an unprecedented willingness to help Tibetan refugees, two cultures came together: Austrians and Tibetans, the two 'small mountain peoples', as the Dalai Lama has repeatedly pointed out. Thousands of kilometres apart and yet so similar in so many ways.

Amala Jetsun Pema, together with the SOS Children's Village headquarters, has provided accommodation, food, education, teachers, foster-mothers and professional vision, as well as funding for this aid project that will last almost a lifetime! I would call her the mother of all European NGOs, or a 'Tibetan Mother Teresa'. She deserves the Nobel Peace Prize as much as her brother.

This reminds me of an equally impressive figure at the time of the Tibetan refugee wave. Indian prime minister Jawaharlal Nehru, leader of the world's largest democratic nation and father of equally legendary Indira Gandhi, supported the Tibetan exodus in 1959 like no other. It was he who gave the Dalai Lama and his people a small hill in the foothills of the Himalayas to settle in: McLeodganj, the then Indian township a few kilometres above present-day Dharamshala. This was at a time when India's partition was already causing enough problems and opposition at home.

Now, over seventy years later, some 25,000 Tibetans live in Dharamshala, gratefully close to their living god. And even the Tibetan government-in-exile resides in this former mountain village. Admirers, friends and supporters of Tibetan culture and religion travel to the region from all over the world. I too have called Dharamshala my second home for almost twenty-five years and have made many Tibetan and Indian friends in the area. The concern that our European generosity and willingness to help the many refugees from Africa and the Middle East is not quite as peaceful as that of the Tibetans is probably justified. One of the main reasons for the non-violent coexistence with the Tibetan refugees is probably the peaceful faith of the Buddhist religion. But the remarkable ability of the Tibetans to integrate gratefully into their country of refuge, while maintaining and preserving their millennia-old culture, is also exemplary.

As early as 1960, after the Dalai Lama had fled, the Swiss government generously offered help and asylum to 300 Tibetan children. A further 150 children were adopted by Swiss citizens. Today, there is a very successful, peaceful community of over 4,000 members of the Tibetan ethnic group in the Swiss mountains.

Although Tibetans tend to live in extended families, village communities are usually even more important than relatives in the mountain villages of the Himalayas. Children separated from their families still benefit from such a system in the SOS Children's Villages, which are also far apart.

I still remember how, years ago, I rented a house in Linz for twenty-five Tibetan refugees, their children and their mothers, so that they could live together. Today, these Tibetans are well integrated. They respect our culture and practise it with an unparalleled consistency, which is something that I often miss in our Austrian families! Our supposedly progressive Europe could learn a lot from these people who were driven from their homeland—charity and tolerance, cultivating one's own culture, respect for parents and the wise and experienced elders, as well as gratitude and attentiveness towards people who are willing to help!

All over the world, political leaders have been destroying whole societies in order to preserve their own cultures and religions. They take control of aeroplanes and try to impose their will by bombing. They will use any means to draw attention to their cause. But their fanatical terror brings nothing but grief and suffering to the people—and usually to their own people.

The Dalai Lama, on the other hand, has succeeded in forbidding his people to resort to violence. Despite being in exile, suffering constant violence at the hands of the Chinese occupiers, Tibetans are strictly forbidden to use violence to draw attention to their situation. The fact that the words of a spiritual leader have such an effect is exemplary in the world—a great attitude to emulate.

If any blood has been shed since then, it has been the blood of Tibetans themselves. More than 160 monks and ordinary Tibetans have died in recent years by self-immolation, by setting themselves on fire to draw attention to the suffering of their people!

May the 'Tibetan Refugees in India' project, started by the wonderful 'Mother of Tibet', find equally wonderful imitators in our Europe.

Tasi delek (a form of Tibetan greeting), Mrs Amala, it was an honour meeting you!

17

'Ibiza Boy' or the Spanish Reincarnation

Once again, I went with some friends to visit Jakob, who lived with his family in the Himalayan mountains high above Dharamshala. We sat on the verandah of his mountain farm and listened intently to his stories. Jakob asked, 'Do you want to go to Lama Thubten Yeshe's teachings this afternoon? He is a very famous reincarnation!'

No one responded. My friends continued to chat about shares and the dollar exchange rate, rather uninterestedly. Jakob, noticing that no one was taking him up on his offer, changed the subject.

During a short break, however, I asked Jakob again about his offer. 'Who is this monk and what special Buddhist rebirth is this about?' I asked curiously. Jakob told me in detail about a rare white European reincarnation, the discovery of which had caused a great stir in the media in the 1990s. I listened with great interest!

In the early 1970s, a Spanish couple, Hannah and Ole Nydahl, travelled to India and Nepal in search of spiritual experiences. Just like today, many dropouts and hippies were travelling to Goa and to the Nepalese capital Kathmandu.

There were not many well-trained Tibetan lamas, and only a few managed to persuade the flower children away from hashish and towards regular Buddhist meditation, much like our Catholic missionaries.

Lama Thubten Yeshe was one of them. He attracted many people with his extroverted, humorous but also engaging personality. After returning home, some of his Western disciples founded Buddhist centres in their home countries, which are internationally networked in the Foundation for the Preservation of the Mahayana Tradition (FPMT).

Lama Thubten's disciple Lama Zopa, who later became the head of the FPMT, was amazed by his mentor's unconventional way of life when he travelled abroad. Even in Hong Kong, the monk would show up at a nightclub in a suit and tie to observe how people spent their time.

In the casino city of Las Vegas, he tried his hand at gambling, and in San Francisco, he happily joined the gay and lesbian parade. Lama Thubten wanted to not only share the teachings of Tibetan Buddhism but also understand the sometimes-extreme lifestyles of his Western students.

Lama Thubten did not hide the fact that he had a serious heart condition. He was particularly fond of Spain. He repeatedly announced predictions in front of a couple, who looked after one of his organisation's meditation centres near Granada, that he would spend a lot of time here in the future. A few months later he died in the USA at the age of forty-nine. Just over a year later, a Spanish couple, María Torres and Paco Hital, had a son, whom they named Ösel (meaning 'clear light' in Tibetan). The birth of their child was followed by dreams in which their Tibetan teacher kept appearing.

Little Ösel was just fourteen months old when Lama Zopa Rinpoche took him to India for tests. As he recognised objects from Lama Thubten Yeshe's former possessions and old acquaintances, it soon became clear that the young Spaniard Ösel Torres must be the 'Tulku', the reincarnation of the beloved, headstrong Tibetan teacher. Even the Dalai Lama eventually confirmed his reincarnation as a high-ranking Gelugpa Buddhist monk and received him several times.

Many Buddhists in the East and West had high hopes for him. Ösel was one of the few westerners to undergo rigorous, traditional Tibetan monastic training. But expectations regarding him succeeding the famous Lama Thubten Yeshe (1935–84) one day were not fulfilled. The young Spaniard turned his back on being a lama, perhaps forever.

But what happened to the official reincarnation of the famous Buddhist lama? At the age of four, he arrived at the Tibetan exile monastery of Sera in southern India to be trained, dressed in precious robes, placed on a throne and worshipped. He was deprived of many things that boys his age in Europe takes for granted. 'Lama Thubten Yeshe was an incredibly hardworking teacher, especially in the West,' said Ösel, recollecting. 'I was taught according to the curriculum of my home country, but my only contact with the West was through films.'

Over the years, his father spent a lot of time in his neighbourhood. The few trips he was allowed to make to Spain left him with impressions that were hard to digest. 'When I left the monastery for two or three weeks, I was mostly passed around the Buddhist centres and had only a few days with my family, whom I hardly knew.' Neither his father nor the monastery, which did not want to lose its great hope for the future, responded to his pleas to be allowed to leave.

When he came of age, he soon packed his bags without having completed his Buddhist training and returned to Spain because he no longer fitted into this life. 'It got in the way of my self-discovery, because it was a lie for me to be there and live [through] something that was imposed on me from the outside.'

Returning to a real European life must have been difficult. The young man had never seen a kissing couple, and his first visit to a smoky discotheque would be a culture shock. But Ösel travelled around, found his feet and discovered his passion for film-making by studying at the Madrid Film Academy. Today, he wears his hair long, plays in a band and loves reggae music.

Even though he has not been able to fulfil the expectations placed on his shoulders, the young *tulku* (meaning reincarmatin in Tibetan) is grateful for getting to experience different cultures in life. Ösel spoke thoughtfully as he summed up what he had to convey: 'The literal translation of lama is teacher, and I am not a teacher. A good lama is someone who doesn't care what others think of him and who thinks of others before himself.'

This young Spaniard, who at the time was jokingly referred to in the media as 'Ibiza Boy', was actually in my neighbourhood and I wanted to take the opportunity to see him and attend his talk. My friends had gone back to their accommodation for lack of interest. Jakob, his wife and I went to the small monastery in a forest clearing just outside Dharamshala. We were a little late; it was raining a bit and the clean monastery complex, run mainly by Buddhist nuns, was packed.

About 300 pairs of shoes, which the visitors had taken off as a precaution to keep the temple clean, were lined up outside the entrance. As I entered, I immediately noticed that the speaker was not there yet. The small throne in the centre of the large hall was still empty. I found a place to sit at the edge of the temple hall and, watching the guests, sat down on the floor like everyone else. They were mainly young people, many of whom had probably travelled especially for the occasion. It was spring and the rhododendrons were in bloom in the mountains around Dharamshala. It was a sight to behold, with the entire Himalayan slopes adorned in a blaze of vivid scarlet blossoms. It was the time before the monsoons, when people from the south fled the heat to the cool mountains.

A nun told us not to take pictures, not to post on Facebook and to switch off our mobile phones during the talk. The monastery hall was packed to the rafters—a strange, whispering crowd waiting for the white guru from Spain.

Right next to me, in front of the large, gilded Buddha statue, I noticed an obvious newcomer. Young, in his late twenties, he had thrown himself full length on the ground in front of the statue as he entered in an extraordinary way—resting his head on the ground, pausing briefly, then standing up and folding his hands with impressive devotion and dignity, greeting the Buddha.

I had often seen Buddhist monks, lamas and the usually very devout Tibetan pilgrims worshipping their idols. This young man, wearing Western jeans, was doing so with remarkable dignity.

After paying homage, he turned and sat down on the small, elaborately embroidered and decorated throne in the centre of the monastery room, adjusted the prepared microphones and greeted the pilgrims present there.

Yes, it was the eagerly awaited reincarnation of Lama Thubten Yeshe, the Spaniard Ösel Hita Torres. A handsome, rakish man with long, glossy black hair, carefully combed back, with a three-day beard.

As the cover boy of any international men's magazine, he could certainly make many a woman's heart beat faster. He greeted us in an unexpectedly soft, calm voice, smiling slightly and speaking in English, which even I understood relatively well.

He began with, 'What do you want to know about me?' He soon explained his life story, his training with the monks at Sera Monastery and his current views about Buddhism in a quick but pleasant, almost casual way. I tried to take notes as he spoke. I jotted down the essence of his experiences in keywords as the crowd listened intently to his stories:

'As long as we don't let go, we are bound. I feel what I feel, but to feel what you feel, you have to communicate. The first form of communication is to listen!

'From the moment we are born, we learn. But the best way to learn is together! The dharma (the Buddhist path) begins with the simplest form of essence, the nectar of "learning".

'The first thing is survival. Most problems and anger come from our ego. So learn to observe yourself! When I get angry, the first question is: Why am I angry?

'Basically, everyone has a good heart, but many people can't open it. As Apple founder Steve Jobs said, "Love is everywhere, not just between mother and child."

'We usually want more than what we have! If we have fresh water, then we want tea, then wine and then champagne ... unfortunately, it's never enough.

'There is no old or new way, there is only one way. You have to find your way, there are so many. Filter your way, find out what is good for you, what helps you. Everyone is different, and that's what's beautiful and special about our lives.

'Learn to listen to your heart. We always want to control everything, and that's not the point. Learn to control yourself, and only then will you gain real strength. Maintaining equilibrium is the right way. Direct everything towards the positive.

'This planet is our school class and we are the students. Ask yourself how you can practise all of what you learn ... make mistakes, forgive yourself and learn from them! I wait after a mistake, think and try to learn ... that makes me wiser. Whenever I fall, I learn and become stronger [...]

'In Tibet, you don't look your teacher in the eye, you look at the ground. And in the West, it's different.'

Asked if he felt like a reincarnation, he replied: 'I feel good. I'm living my life now, I didn't feel that years ago, but now I do ... My mission is not to become a teacher, it is to pass on Buddhism, to bring it to people who don't know about it yet. My parents were Buddhists. It was difficult for them to give up their child, many were unhappy when I left the monastery. Now they understand why I came back ... As a monk, I learnt discipline in everyday life when I left. I didn't know what to do.

'My first trip was to a disco, it was loud, smoky, you couldn't talk, you couldn't listen. When I wanted a coke, the man at the bar asked me: "With whisky or rum?"

'I said, "Does it matter?"

'When I danced, I moved only slightly, as I had learnt and practised in the monastery. Everyone laughed and after a few minutes, I was out of the disco ... Believe me, I have had many girls. I partied with boys and millionaires, I attended a lot of parties, I learnt to step on the gas, I took drugs, and remembered next to nothing the day after! I soon realized that maintaining equilibrium is the way to go.

'We should thank our planet! The planet is not here for us, the planet is our school, we are the pupils ... The problem is oil, cement, dynamite, but it's not too late.

'Practise Buddhism, only humans can practise it, not animals.'

I had only intended to stay a few minutes to take some good photographs of the reincarnate, but I stayed until the last minute of his teaching. I was fascinated by the young, cosmopolitan Spaniard and envied him for this training in his short life.

On my way out, I bowed deeply in admiration, and we looked into each other's eyes for a long time, as a special person should, or as we westerners have learnt to do.

His teachings and words will stay with me for the rest of my life, giving me the strength to endure the daily lows of the constant Western struggle, to be able to forgive, to achieve the great goal of balance again and again, and to gain energy for new tasks. He has already begun his journey to bring the teachings of Buddhism to the Western world. Does he realise that he has already taken up the legacy of Lama Thubten Yeshe?

18

Managers in the Himalayas

Friends who run huge companies with thousands of employees have been regular guests at my inn for many years. We share the pleasure of having good wine and good food.

Time and again, my friendship and work with Tibetan refugee children have been the subject of our long and enjoyable evenings. 'Of course, you should come with us to the refugee children, to Tibet. That shouldn't be a problem!'

I would usually smile and add: 'I hope it works out one day.'

Now the time had come. I wanted to take them to the foothills of the Himalayas, to the places I had first visited some twenty-five years ago. I had often accompanied some kind people with me, friends and supporters of my Josef Tibet Project. There were only a few of them whom I had contacted myself; it was always important to me that the people I was travelling with understood that it involved actual endeavour and was not merely another tick off on an empty slot on the

'TripAdvisor' list. I also wanted to be sure that the culture and beliefs of my Tibetan friends would be respected. Travellers who have the privilege of being taught the principles of an ancient culture by Tibetans who have been driven from their homeland should, above all, be grateful, sensitive and attentive.

I still remember, with horror, about a director who had a special talent for putting her foot in her mouth. I had supported her and her camera team financially to enable them to make a film about the escape and life of Tibetan children in exile. A situation such as this would require at least a little sensitivity, especially because they were dealing with traumatised children. Unfortunately, the sensationalist woman lacked this completely. In order to emphasise the tension and suffering of the girls and boys, she kept asking them about their arduous, endless journey over the snow-covered mountains of the Himalayas in minute detail, until the children burst into terrible fits of crying. 'Quick, close-up, go,' the director shouted to her cameraman as she tried to intensify the crying with her interrogative questions. The desired emotions brought ratings.

It did not go down well with me. At first, I was a little distracted while playing with the Tibetan children outside the orphanage, when I heard the sobs of the girl being interviewed. I quickly realised what was happening. Arguing was not my thing. But now that I knew what the director was up to, I decided to stop contacting her about her 'stories'.

Unfortunately, this only made things worse. She then went off on her own, trying to get interviews with the Dalai Lama, his sister Jetsun Pema and other senior Tibetan dignitaries. It wasn't the wisest thing to do, of course, but everyone defends themselves in their own way—they in their own way, I in mine.

After almost twenty-five years of friendship, I was well acquainted with the people she approached, and so I received several phone calls a day asking about the 'action-hungry' wishes of the 'camera lady' I had brought with me. I watched with barely concealed pleasure as my Tibetan friends explained to her in a very polite and friendly manner that the desired interviewees were very busy and that they would get back to her as soon as the opportunity arose. She never heard a 'no'. The 'maybe tomorrow' was my Tibetan friends' cautious attempt to put something off forever without ever having to say no directly.

My travel companion eventually ran out of time and her film consisted mainly of footage of the beautiful region. The story ended mainly with interview clips of Tibetans living in Austria.

Back to the trip with my manager friends. After almost twelve hours in the air, the real adventure began with a five-hour train journey by the Shatabdi Express from Delhi to Kalka, a small town just behind Chandigarh, at the foot of the Himalayan massif at about 650 metres above sea level.

The Delhi railway station was spectacular when we arrived. Anyone who has ever walked into an Indian railway station in the early hours of the morning will know what I'm talking about. To catch the endless trains that leave in the early hours of the morning, hundreds of people sleep on the concrete slabs warmed by the day's heat. For my friends who were experiencing this for the first time, it was undoubtedly a terrible culture shock.

I must admit that my blood pressure always peaks when I try to find the platform, track, train, carriage and seat on the hard-to-read tickets. However, having once discovered that the train I had pre-booked was delayed by a whole day (!), I have been prepared for anything when entering an Indian railway station ever since!

We had taken four porters with us—and also kept a low profile as a precaution—to help carry our luggage and to help us find our way to the destination as we were not very familiar with the area. Once again, we could see dozens of people lying on the ground on cardboard boxes covered with blankets. It was hard to tell if anyone would wake them up to get them on the right train. We couldn't miss the many rats eating the discarded food about a metre down between the tracks.

Anyway, we boarded the train, wisely following the porters. As if controlled by an invisible hand, the Gordian knot at the station had been untied and we were relieved to be in the right seats. A generous tip for the porters was in order, and we were immediately handed some much-needed mineral water bottles. Instead of exploring the Indian countryside through the morning mist, I sank into the pleasant rumble of the Shatabdi Express and was on our way to Kalka.

My fellow travellers had also fallen asleep. Soon we were awakened by the friendly, grinning Indian conductor. Sleepy and tired, we grabbed our luggage from the racks and exited the train in an unnecessary hurry.

The legendary snorting and smoking Toy Train, with its carriages that looked more like a miniature railway, was already waiting opposite its big, speeding brother, the Shatabdi Express. The English had built the Toy Train in the mid-nineteenth century. Then, as now, it was used during the hot summer months to escape the monsoon heatwave and go to the cooler mountains. Because of its spectacular and sometimes dangerous route, it became a popular tourist destination, which is certainly not the reason why it was declared a UNESCO World Heritage Site in 2008. In any case, the railway would take us to the hill station, Shimla, founded by the British in the Himalayas at an altitude of around 2,000 metres. The Toy Train travels through 164 tunnels in five hours, often being overtaken by large numbers of cyclists. Yes, that's how slowly this old, lovable monster makes its way through the Himalayan foothills.

I was sitting at the exit, my feet hanging down, with the carriage doors open. I was happily distributing the Josef balloons I had bought to the generally amiable Indian youngsters who were playing and waving.

Some thoughts were constantly running through my mind: What would the journey with my westernised top managers amount to? How would it end? Was a fight inevitable? Would we still be friends after this trip? I had been carrying these thoughts since long before our company. All of these friends were powerful managers. Hans was on the board of Deutsche Bahn, a company with almost 300,000 employees. Roland was one of the leading CEOs of an international American company with around 35,000 employees, and Klaus had just become a victim of one of the many restructuring measures of the perpetually loss-making Austrian Federal Railways, but he was still a manager. He, with his eternally restless nature, was not ready for a hasty retirement—would he find peace where we were going?

I had provided my companions with plenty of information about our trip: vaccination schedules, packing lists, codes of conduct and so on.

During one of our evenings together, I explained the 'Himalayan Code' in detail. It was extremely important to respect the different ancient cultures and customs, so I emphasised the importance of our behaviour towards these people. The population there was going through a rapid process of change, and it was up to us to be understanding and not create any more uncertainty, I told them.

It remained to be seen whether they understood my information, whether they had thought about it and whether they would be able to show the necessary sensitivity towards these cultures.

Throughout the long journey, they kept telling me about expensive management seminars in the most beautiful places in the world, about modern gurus trying to teach them about team spirit and leadership skills for exorbitant sums of money. They were the ones who provided work and a fair income for hard-working employees. They decided the social fate of thousands of people. Yet they were among the managers who were constantly criticised in our affluent Europe. Of course, it was their job to ensure that their companies made juicy profits. At the same time, however, they were 'partly to blame' for the ever-widening gap between rich and poor on our continent.

In any case, I hoped it would be an exciting 'seminar trip' to experience the cultures of the Himalayas and to visit people who for thousands of years have dedicated themselves to the exploration of human spiritual science, the exploration of our inner selves. I was almost a little scared, and I noticed my blood pressure rising again, despite my Buddhist serenity. I couldn't help but think of the words of a famous lama: 'Only by mastering great tasks can you learn and develop.' In the hierarchy of these top managers, the best I could hope for was a managerial position in the staff canteen of their huge companies. So, I was quite curious to see if they would be willing to follow my path.

I was jolted out of my dream by the horrified words from Klaus: 'Look at these filthy pigs! So much rubbish on both sides of the railway! It looks like a garbage dump!' Then he took a deep breath and immediately launched into an all-out attack: 'They should come to Europe ... they could learn how to separate their rubbish!'

Worried, I searched for what he was pointing at and looked outside. Countless tourists had left a veritable garbage dump on both sides of the railway tracks on the busy route. The mountains of discarded trash were disgusting and horrible to look at, and sadly, for all to see, much of the discarded goods had been once imported by Western companies. Neither the Indian tourists nor the locals have understood that plastic and aluminium packaging do not automatically decompose in nature like the banana leaves or simple paper that have been used for generations.

Although the Indian authorities and numerous environmental organisations are constantly striving to avoid these mountains of waste, they are no match for the carefree tourists who arrive in droves from large Indian cities. It is the same problem that first baffled us in Europe in the 1970s and '80s, one that we have still not managed to get under control.

Himachal Pradesh, the northern Indian mountain state, passed a law banning the use of plastic bags more than ten years ago. The many tourists frequenting the state know about it but seem to ignore it. Tourists bring money, and the people are usually very friendly to them. Pointing out the carelessness of 'guests' is (unfortunately) against Indian politeness.

Wandering sacred cows feed on the plastic waste and perish. All too often, their carcasses can be seen on the side of the roads, serving as food for stray dogs and vultures.

How short-sighted and inconsiderate can we be to disparage someone's culture. We, in Europe, have struggled for almost a century with mechanical technology to keep the streets reasonably clean and tidy. Everything takes time. So why should we not give these people a few more years to get a grip on the waste they (and we) have brought in? But no, I'd better not explain all this to Klaus...

He probably wouldn't (want to) understand that a lot has already changed for the better in Delhi. I can still remember the old Delhi—thousands of people sleeping on the roadside, sacred cows making it dangerous to drive in the city centre, elephants roaming freely in the parks, and crowds of beggars knocking on car windows at crossroads, begging for money or food.

I am always annoyed when I come home and see crowds of professional beggars in our upmarket shopping streets. These are young, healthy men begging for money while working full-time. Do-gooders affected by our capitalist affluence promote and encourage this, whereas in India, initiatives such as 'Clean Delhi Green Delhi' are used to encourage beggars to do their part for a cleaner India. Smoking is already banned in all public places, streets and gardens in India. Yes, Delhi can already compete with the big cities of Asia in many aspects, and people are trying very hard to realise this possibility. Over the last twenty-five years, I have noticed positive changes.

We finally arrived at Shimla railway station. Mohit, my friend of many years, greeted us, beaming with joy. Up on the steep slopes of the Himalayan foothills, we were surrounded by a dense crowd amid the shouting and haggling of porters. For a measly hundred Indian rupees (about 1.20 euros), old, bearded, tanned porters dragged our suitcases up countless steps to the waiting jeep. I could hardly believe it! One of my friends even started haggling with the porter. He did not wish to pay more than 50 rupees (about 0.60 euros) for his two suitcases, which weighed at least 35 kilograms. It was just embarrassing for me.

I recalled the last argument I had had with my airline's check-in desk in Vienna when they refused to take my suitcase that was weighing 24 kilograms. The staff at Vienna airport couldn't be expected to handle more than 21 kilograms. I had to repack and pay for the excess baggage.

As usual, I surreptitiously slipped the porter a hundred rupee note, and once again received a friendly smile—that saved my day.

Shortly afterwards, I looked around at frowning faces—the fully packed jeep offered very little space for its passengers. Yes, it's true, that in Austria it would probably only have been registered for four people. But in India, you just load it until every inch of space is used. The reason is simple; it's the only way to save expensive petrol. But that's a good point!

As a guide who knew the area, I was entitled to the front seat next to the driver. Mohit and my three friends shared the back seat of the old jeep. We had to stow all our luggage between our feet, in the back and on the roof. I can't remember who asked the quiet question if this was the jeep we would be travelling in for the next few days. My answer was: 'Yes, of course', accompanied by a barely perceptible smile on my face.

We were staying at Woodville Palace. The venerable hotel once belonged to the Raja of Jhalawar, who ruled over a vast kingdom in the Himalayas. I had chosen this hotel because it always reminded me of our venerable Emperor Franz Joseph I's summer holidays in Bad Ischl. That is how I imagined the Villa Schratt, where the Habsburg ruler enjoyed his Gugelhupf with his mistress.

Tiger heads, prepared as hunting trophies, hung on the walls next to photographs of famous Hollywood stars who had once been guests at the hotel. The Indian sentry greeted us as if the British viceroy himself had arrived. It had been a long day. We had travelled ten hours by train, sat in cramped spaces, climbed 2,000 metres and finally arrived in the state capital of Himachal Pradesh.

Mohit and his wife Seema had invited us to a local restaurant for dinner and were to pick us up in an hour. So, I had a quick shower, changed into fresh clothes and joined my friends in the hotel's Bollywood-themed bar for an Indian Kingfisher beer.

Judging by their faces, they were in no mood to enjoy themselves. I was met with a rather reproachful look. There was only cold water in the room, the boiler was broken, what about athlete's foot; and where could one get their dirty laundry washed—these were just some of the questions asked at the bar.

I knew that Aditya, my friend, the Maharaja of Kangra, knew the venerable owner of the hotel very well and had asked him to announce our arrival. The hotel porter then forwarded us a personal invitation from the hotel owner and former king of Jhalawar. The next day, just before we left, we were told that His Highness would like to receive us in his private chambers. What an honour!

But now I was really looking forward to meeting Seema, the beautiful wife of Mohit, my long-time friend and companion on so many trips to the Tibetan border in the Himalayas.

She worked in Shimla as a German teacher for the Goethe-Institut—which was always a welcome relief for me with my poor English—and Mohit also spoke German very well.

Klaus was the self-appointed jester in our group. We always had a lot of fun with him around. Sometimes, I couldn't stop laughing at his jokes. Unfortunately, there were times he trampled on our company like an Indian elephant, demanding attention without consideration. We laughed at Klaus's bad German–English jokes and the evening passed without what I felt was a necessary discussion about the rest of our journey. Even after that, meaningful communication between friends was not possible. Unfortunately, this was not to be without consequences.

Mohit had arranged for us to play golf nearby. Shimla claims to have come up with the first golf course in Asia. It was carved into the Himalayan mountains by the British in 1905. From the laughter of the local caddies, it was clear that I wasn't very good at it, but it was worth it to play a round of golf in mountain boots, under the careful protection of an Indian soldier. He wasn't carrying the rifle loaded with heavy lead shot as a mere decoration. There are plenty of bears and mountain leopards in the area.

On the way back from my adventurous golfing trip, I wanted to visit the Nyingmapa Buddhist monastery in Shimla. We soon found it, perched on the southern slope. The golden roofs dazzled us in the sun. It was the first Tibetan monastery my friends had seen on our tour through the mountains of northern India. I thought I saw a little fear cloud Klaus's face. Buddhist serenity, calmness and letting go were not his strong points. He was always the one drawing attention to himself with jokes and banter. His strengths probably wouldn't have been of much use to him there. In any case, he seemed rather insecure as he entered the monastery grounds.

We were greeted politely. At first, they didn't pay much attention to us. It was only when I showed the monks my photographs of His Holiness and myself that they began to whisper and point at me. They bowed respectfully to me, and more and more monks came running to see the 'friend of the Dalai Lama'.

I asked for the Rinpoche, the abbot of the monastery. I was asked to follow some of the monks. In a large square, just below the large monastery, we saw a big, white, beautifully decorated stupa around which an old, frail monk was being wheeled in a wheelchair. Many monks followed him, slightly bent over, full of respect and humility.

It was Rinpoche. He was visibly very ill. As I approached, he smiled and gave me a Tibetan welcome shawl.

The abbot's voice was very soft. One of the monks told me he was pleased to welcome a good acquaintance of Rigo Tulku. I also bowed and smiled at him.

The Rinpoche, I was later told, had been in Ladakh and, like so many people, had endured serious problems with altitude sickness. He had therefore left at short notice and returned to his monastery to recuperate.

This was certainly a happy coincidence for me—another new acquaintance in my long list of great Buddhist teachers in faraway northern India.

Over a hearty breakfast, we discussed at length the question of travelling north or south as an extension of our tour. I listened to my manager friends for a while and smiled to myself.

Having everything under control and always knowing where we were going—this was the best description of my job. I had already explained the complete itinerary in detail to my friends back home, even drawing it on a map. But none of them had it with them! Harbouring the unrealistic belief that we could go ahead with the journey by relying on Google maps, they had left the detailed itinerary and map at home. To this day, I still don't understand how anyone could think that there would always be sufficient Internet connections up in the Himalayas.

For me, the map wasn't that important. I just trusted the driver, as I always do. He knew exactly where and how to drive. On my last few journeys, the route had to be changed all too often due to bad weather, broken bridges and mudslides. The climate changes are evident at every turn. The largest mountain range in the world, the Himalayas, is not static in one place. It continues to move inexorably, and with that comes the change.

Monsoons, which used to be eagerly awaited once, is now arriving earlier and earlier than the expected dates, with incessant rain. It softens the makeshift wooden and mud huts, like doll's houses, until they too fall victim to the floods.

These thoughts crossed my mind while Roland lectured me at the breakfast table, his gaze intently concentrated on me: 'You're not relaxed, Günter. You're far too busy—do you want to know why?' He could obviously see the answer in the look I gave him. He immediately qualified his warning, which was earlier seeming more of a threat: 'Then don't,' he said, got up and left.

I couldn't believe it. These stress-ridden top managers, who would have loved to be travelling around northern India, relying on Google Maps, carrying a laptop, and who knew only the pressure of deadlines, had nothing better to do than talk all day about shares, company sales and team building. It didn't occur to them to study the philosophy and culture of the people of the place they were visiting. They accused me, of all people, of being busy, when I was probably the only one with the pulse of a sleeping cat. Well, that's nothing new, it's always someone else's fault.

I had arrived in the Himalayas body and mind. I had long since swapped my mobile phone for an Indian one, to be able to communicate with the driver and my Tibetan friends.

Tso Pema, the Holy Lake

We were on our way to Tso Pema, the sacred lake high up in the mountains where probably the most famous reincarnation of the Dalai Lama, 'Padmasambhava', is said to have lived in the eighth century and meditated in a cave for years. All locals knew about the story of his forbidden marriage to the daughter of a powerful local raja.

Today, thousands of Buddhists and Hindus make a pilgrimage to this remote mountain settlement and circle the small romantic lake in a clockwise direction, often several times a day and even at night. For a long time, I refused to even mention the name of this wonderful hidden gem in my travel reports. Unfortunately, social media forums and Google were less sensitive.

Instead of enjoying our extraordinary experiences, the unnecessary discussion about a 'much-needed' map became increasingly heated. It wasn't the beautiful area that was interesting to them—no, my manager friends wanted to know whether we were travelling north or south.

Marvelling at my Buddhist composure, I interrupted the heated discussion with the worst argument my fellow travellers had ever heard—that the map was completely insignificant!

It only took a few seconds for my three friends to attack me. They accused me of being nonsensical and added that I should have instead made sure to carry a map. In their defence, they said they could have possibly not known that Google maps wouldn't work there.

But in my mind, I had disarmed those managers—unconsciously, of course. They were 'control freaks'. But now with no map, they had no control over the situation! Defenceless, they were forced to trust our driver and my leadership. An undeniable fact, but one they were unable to deal with properly.

The first conflict was on its way.

My friends tried to take the lead themselves. They stopped the driver at every little roadside hut and asked for what seemed to be an extremely important road map. Unsuccessfully, of course, but to my secret delight.

When the driver kindly pointed out that we would be arriving at our destination in about twenty minutes, my newly self-appointed 'leadership team' once again showed their mental strength. Although the destination of our eight-hour journey was at last visible to the naked eye, they stopped the jeep again for a much-needed short rest.

The three self-appointed leaders had one thing on their minds: we'd lost far too much time and still had no place to stay. I could only hope that we would still have a chance of finding accommodation before nightfall—not just any accommodation, of course, but one with reasonably clean rooms. That would have given us plenty of time to relax afterwards. But this was all about power games, so unfortunately common sense fell by the wayside.

The accommodation problem was not so easy to solve. My old Tibetan friend Norgyal Choephel was spending his well-earned retirement there. I rang him and asked him to find us a clean guest house.

At last, we found accommodation in an old and dirty monastery. Our dingy rooms were on the second floor. The sheets had probably been washed countless times and were full of stains and holes. The windows had makeshift bars because of the many monkeys who stole anything and everything that wasn't locked up.

When we asked for hot water, we were informed that the solar water-heating system was broken, so we had to make do with ice-cold water. As a precautionary measure, we were carrying a crate of beer. We met in my room for a reconciliation drink, which ended in a big binge.

We'd brought enough whisky with us as an everyday 'disinfectant', but unfortunately, we didn't have any glasses.

Klaus solved this problem by cutting a plastic water bottle into half to make two sealed containers, which we ended up using as drinking vessels. Tap water replaced the usual tonic. There was no ice, but the cold water made up for that.

Again, the dirt on the roadsides, the musty accommodation and the dirty toilets on the streets became the main topics of our discussions. In the end, however, we enjoyed the cigars we had brought with us and lost ourselves in endless debates on more or less fruitful topics.

Eventually, we all fell asleep in rooms that had been turned into smoking rooms by the cigar smoke.

I woke up early and tried to do the *kora*, walking on the pilgrimage route around the holy lake in the morning. I just wanted to be alone, introspect and enjoy the silence. The kora always involves walking in a clockwise direction. However, I came across my three friends who had also decided to perform kora and were about to walk around the lake anticlockwise— which the many pilgrims around did not correct but accepted with a slight smile.

Thankfully, peace had returned, but—as I was soon to discover—only for a short time. The claims to leadership had not been settled.

My friends and I had travelled far into the mountains above Tso Pema in our jeep. We soon noticed the prayer flags pointing the way to the entrance of the cave. We crossed paths marked with colourful prayer flags waving in the light breeze. Before entering the cave, Buddhist nuns told us we had to take off our shoes. Klaus refused. He did not want to risk getting athlete's foot. So while the rest of us set off to explore the mysterious, millennia-old cave, with its giant Buddha statues, he remained demonstratively seated at the entrance.

I had bought some tallow candles from the nuns and lit them in the small old temple attached to the cave. Yes, I hummed 'Our Father', a Christian prayer. I was sure that Buddha, Shiva and Jesus Christ would understand me. I had not learnt how to speak Tibetan yet.

We drove back a little pensive. I noticed that my friends were impressed by everything they had seen. The evening passed very quietly, and we soon went to bed—after all, we had another long journey ahead of us the next day.

Management Meeting or a Beer in Bir

Early the next morning, we set off on a three-hour jeep drive to Dharamshala. Our next stop was Bir, a small but remarkable Indian village.

The journey took us along the foothills of the Himalayas at around 2,000 metres above sea level. Some of the roads, painstakingly carved into the steep slopes, were easily motorable, with some being tarred. We were constantly passing by construction sites and seemed to be stuck in never-ending queues of vehicles. Eventually, the roads, which had been destroyed by mudslides, were bulldozed back into service. We were often accompanied by miles of tea gardens along the roadside. It was a joy and a feast for the eyes to watch the proud and colourfully dressed tea pickers as they filled their baskets on their backs with the precious Himalayan tea leaves and waved to us in a friendly manner. I had once again brought countless Josef balloons, which I released from my car for the children playing by the roadside. I could still see their white teeth gleaming in the rear-view mirror as they waved gratefully. This would usually end in a wild scramble and heated arguments, with the strongest kid usually winning.

We crossed more and more torrential meltwater rivers. Their ice-cold waters thunderously joined the Beas in the vast Kangra Valley and then the equally mighty Sutlej, which was dammed by the Pong Dam to generate electricity. I told my companions that it was the family of Maharaja Aditya Katoch, the former king of Kangra, and his father who had built this enormous structure. They also initiated the construction of a canal more than a thousand kilometres long in distant Rajasthan to bring precious water to the people there in the desert.

Today, some 400 tonnes of fish are caught each year in this unique water reserve by some 2,000 local fishermen. It is also one of the largest bird sanctuaries in the world. Millions of migratory birds wait here before flying back across the Himalayas during spring to their breeding grounds in distant Mongolia, Siberia and China.

The water from the Pong Dam is eventually taken over by the mighty and sacred Indus River, which rises in the Tibetan highlands and channels the huge masses of water into the Arabian Sea.

I dared to doubt whether my fellow travellers knew that their actions too contributed to the climatic changes in the area in one way or the other. In any case, they showed little interest in learning about it. It is well known that careful management of pollution in our latitudes could help reduce the threat of massive snowmelt in the Himalayas. Experts are already talking of an imminent Third World War, triggered by the struggle for the coveted fruit of water at the top of the world—electricity generation.

I spared myself the trouble of bringing this up for discussion. It was easy to note that my companions were not in the mood for such in-depth discussions that day.

Bir, the Indo-Tibetan village nestled in the picturesque Himalayan foothills of the Kangra Valley, gave us a 'friendly and cheerful' welcome. We could see tea plantations, romantic Indian farms and last winter's snow still glistening on the horizon. It rarely snows in the valley, and temperatures rarely rise above 30 degrees in summer.

The mighty lamas from faraway Tibet have settled in the area. Wealthy Buddhist businessmen from America and Singapore have helped finance monasteries and nowhere else is there such a concentration of monastic universities. Monks and Tibetan families have settled in the surrounding region; three huge SOS Children's Villages for Tibetan refugees have been built here; and in 2006, I opened my first Home Josef in the small neighbouring village of Suja.

We had made a reservation at my friend Rigo Tulku's guest house. They were waiting for us to arrive.

Well, it wasn't a five-star hotel. Personally, I thought it was more like a decent two-star hotel. At least, they always kept it clean, and as the hotel was away from the noisy village road, one could give it a few extra points for its location. A small garden and a café serving pizzas summed up its positive points.

Shortly before midday, we met in the café right after the tour of the rooms. Everyone was looking forward to a cold beer in Bir.

I enjoyed smoking my first cigar and listening to my friends' conversations. Soon, the the topic of discussion shifted to a scheduled meeting with the fifty Tibetan girls from Home Josef. The meeting was to be held in the afternoon, and my manager friends were starting to voice their concern regarding the organisational bits of the meeting.

'Fifty girls! Where are they all going to sit? What will they eat? What will they drink? We don't have enough presents for everyone! How are we going to communicate with them when they only speak Tibetan? And anyway, how much is this going to cost and who is going to pay for it?' These were some of the questions from their lively 'business meeting' up in the Himalayas.

Unimpressed, I continued to puff on my cigar, enjoy my cold beer and smile contentedly to myself. Suddenly, I felt so infinitely light and exhilarated, and as a warming white cloud gently enveloped me, I viewed the world through a different lens.

My manager friends seemed to be at a loss. There was no secretary to provide the seemingly necessary documents, no marketing expert to make appropriate suggestions, no otherwise urgently needed concept to build on or nag about, no indispensable telephone to make a quick enquiry or get the information they needed. I couldn't suppress my laughter anymore. I had disarmed them, these big, powerful managers, helplessly feeling each other out because there was no protocol or programme for inviting the children. I could feel them quivering inside, looking for someone to blame for their helplessness, and yes, their search seemed to end with me once again. 'Tell me,' started one of the gentlemen, 'while we're scratching our heads over how to organise this meeting, you're laughing like you are watching a puppet show? You're sitting there enjoying yourself, drinking your beer and puffing on your cigar. How about you finally getting involved in planning for the meeting with the fifty children? They'll be here in about two hours—and nothing's planned, nothing's organised!'

My three friends looked at me reproachfully. They were helpless, without the usual structures of their companies, disempowered there at the end of the world, without the necessary network to tap into, without an expensive lobbyist always on hand with advice and recommendations. I could feel their helplessness, which was in fact about to turn into a storm, a storm that seemed to be heading in my direction.

Perhaps it wasn't fair on my part not to have told them that I had, of course, sorted things out a few days before we arrived, all by an exchange of emails with the secretary of Rigo Tulku, the head lama. It was simple and the request was very short: 'Dear friend,' I had written, 'as always, I am inviting the children from Home Josef again this year. As always, they will want to eat their beloved momo. Please prepare enough of those. Last year, it was ten per child. Better make a few more this time. As you know, they'll wrap up the rest and take them home.'

Tibetans don't eat meat. So, as every year, there were to be plenty of vegetarian momo and Coca-Cola, of course. Every kid in the world thinks Coke is 'cool'. Up there, the kids literally started clamouring for it.

I couldn't stop laughing, and it was only too late to realise that I had gone a little too far. They had already seen my stoic 'non-participation' in their meeting regarding the invitation as carelessness, but my laughter was considered a 'great insult'. A storm of accusations poured down on me. I had to accept that my corporate friends had held this 'business meeting' in a world of their own, which was distinct from my world in the Himalayas.

They were accustomed to getting suggestions and then making decisions. But I had failed to deliver the same in time. Again, I didn't quite see any reason for them to attack me like that. The organisation of the trip was entirely up to me anyway. So, I took a deep breath and counter-attacked:

'My dear friends, we are not here in the conference room of your office castles, in your mighty control centres. Here, decisions are made based on experience. Age and wisdom take precedence over title and position. If you had absorbed just a little of this knowledge of the local culture and population, you might have realised that I am an innkeeper—and have been since long. It's my everyday job to organise events. Everyone knows that—and so do you. But in your daily obsession with what you do and how you do it, you have forgotten the shortest and easiest way. How about just asking me how things are going with the kids today, or how can we contribute? After a week of "Himalayan Seminar", how come you still haven't learnt?'

In response, I received an uncomfortable silence.

'To put your worries to rest, everything has been organised already. Organised by me, of course! That was my job. But you can still do something. The fifty children will be here in an hour. All we need is some melons from the market in the village. If you want to, you're welcome to. And as a little hint, the children are going to sing for us today. I've promised to play something for them on my pan pipes. So why don't you think about what simple gifts you can offer? Dancing or singing—there are no limits to your imagination.'

I found myself grinning with satisfaction. There was silence across the table. Not a word was spoken. The three of them just looked at me as if I'd just cancelled their management contract without notice. 'Uhhh ... and what's this about dancing and singing ... who? Us?'

They suddenly seemed to be in a hurry to 'get some melons' from the market. But I could overhear them from a distance as they walked away: '... about dancing and singing, he's totally crazy!'

I woke up startled, shaking my head trying to wake up. Had I perhaps fallen asleep ... for a short time? In any case, I took advantage of my friends' absence to decorate the small garden with the hundred Josef balloons I had already kept aside safely. Somehow, I felt the need to give my kids a special treat. With the help of a Tibetan waiter, we assembled a few heavy, rustic wooden tables such that fifty people could be accommodated. I felt it was important that we all sat together at the same table. I checked the momo production in the kitchen. They had made about 600. The vegetable-filled dumplings had been cooked in the wood-burning oven over steaming water. About fifty plates were ready and the Tibetan waiters grinned at me expectantly. They already knew me, as this was not the first party we had organised together for the girls. The girls from Home Josef arrived on time—at the same time as my friends who walked in carrying melons.

Greeting fifty girls in person can be quite exhausting, especially if you want to give each child the same amount of attention. The girls had all turned up in their school uniforms—blue trousers and white shirts, most of which they had sewn themselves. The housemother from Home Josef had seen to it. Tsewang Jeshe, the director of the huge SOS refugee village in Suja, home to around 2,500 Tibetan refugee children, also came. '*Tashi delek, Günter La*—may you be well, Günter,' he greeted me—a very special greeting from a friend.

Of course, I enjoyed the attentive looks of my manager friends. Apparently, they had begun to realise how strong my bond with the Tibetan people was. While the 600 momo and fifty cans of cola were being served, Tsewang Jeshe opened the wonderful children's festival with a short speech. Everyone listened intently. 'Günter La, how nice that you and your friends are visiting us again. How nice that we can be your guests today.' Then he took his plate of momo and began to sing a Tibetan grace. All fifty children joined in with their shrill, high-pitched voices which was so typical of the people living on the roof of the world. As is often the case on such occasions, I couldn't control my emotions and the tears rolled down my eyes. It must have been an inner voice that suddenly remembered a life lived long before this one. An inner voice kept telling me: 'You're one of them—that's what your mum used to sing when she brought your food up here.'

My friends watched me with obvious discomfort. Showing emotion was not an option for them, as emotions had no place in their world. They saw it as a sign of weakness. Successful managers are often very lonely and hard-working, and it is only at the end of their careers that they realise how important this world of emotions and feelings is. It is then that many of them then start seeking fortune in the Himalayas. Unfortunately, it is usually far too late.

At the gathering, the girls were finally able to get their hands on their favourite momo. One couldn't imagine how much they enjoyed and craved the ten pieces of these very satisfying dumplings. Coca-Cola cans were refilled and many of them also rushed over to a table of ripe watermelons.

Perhaps my friends were beginning to realise that joy, happiness and gratitude were the order of the day in an honest emotional world, a world they probably were not familiar with or had long forgotten.

Shortly afterwards, the children wanted to express their gratitude. They had been rehearsing songs and dance performances for weeks. They giggled shyly as if it were their first performance. But then we were treated to a remarkable programme of Tibetan folklore. We got to enjoy Tibetan songs that their parents had sung to them as babies long ago in distant Tibet and dances that recalled their families' harvests in the Himalayas. They always performed with a searching look on their faces to gauge whether we were impressed and satisfied. The young ladies' programme also included the latest songs. Like everywhere else in the world, they too had favourite artists in the world of international music. The songs of Lady Gaga and Michael Jackson had already arrived in Tibet—but the children would never forget the songs of their mothers.

Soon, it was our turn. Roland, the manager of some 20,000 employees, asked me to play an Elvis song on my iPhone, following which he could perform a variation of it, but he failed miserably. Klaus started dancing a polka with one of the girls. That too didn't go well. Finally, it was Hans's turn. He felt obliged to sing the local national anthem, and that added to the disastrous performances. I tried to save the situation by playing Leo Roja's *'Hallelujah'* on my pan pipes. But I didn't quite succeed and had to unfortunately join the ranks of my previously failed friends.

In the end, we were saved by the seemingly unclouded friendliness of the Tibetans. Suddenly, my friends were seen chatting with the children by the light of a candle, animated and unafraid. The spell was broken—the tough-as-nails managers went on asking the children about their arduous and dangerous escape over the snow-covered mountains of the Himalayas. They slowly realised that each of these girls had achieved things that our usually spoilt children only see on television, if at all. But they were able to share a unique evening with the fifty true heroes of the Himalayas.

This time, my friends stood right next to me as we bid goodbye after exchanging handshakes. No one wanted to miss the opportunity to look into the innocent girls' wide, deep black eyes. Later, we retired to bed with a sense of amazement. It seemed to me that my manager friends had finally arrived in the Himalayas and had become thoughtful.

19

Watching the Dalai Lama Teach

Up to 3,000 people usually attend a Dalai Lama teaching in the small township of McLeodganj, which is always held at his Tibetan Buddhist monastery. Such a teaching always makes for a special event. It doesn't matter whether you can follow the Dalai Lama's explanations. Even if the philosophical depth of his view is not fully accessible to everyone, a dense atmospheric aura ensures that his spirit can penetrate deep into the bodies of all those present.

It was early in the morning. The air was filled with the aroma of sweet rolls. From the kitchen came the steady sound of gas flames, pots clattering and a tap dripping. The yellow walls glowed in the first rays of sunlight. An old woman came around the corner. She was wearing a dark brown, floor-length dress that was clearly too big for her. Her long grey hair was braided into two plaits with four bright blue and red ribbons artfully interwoven. Her right hand rested on a wooden walking stick. Her left hand clutched a white package to her chest. Slowly, but purposefully, she approached a young monk whose brow was already beading with sweat early in the day. When she reached him, she held out the parcel without a word. Then she turned away, muttering to herself. The monk took the milk carton and dropped it into a large metal bucket. Dozens of others like that carton were already stacked inside—donations were always welcome.

To make Tibetan butter tea, you need milk, tea, butter and salt. And if you want to feed around 3,000 registered visitors with the nutritious Tibetan national drink, as was the case on the second morning of the Dalai Lama's three-day teaching in Dharamshala, you would need correspondingly large quantities of these ingredients. As admission to the Tibetan religious leader's teachings, which take place several times a year, is free, they rely on money and food donations from sponsors and participants.

Attendees started flocking to the large yellow complex of the world-famous Tsuklakhang Temple, picturesquely situated at the end of a forested ridge almost 2,000 metres high at the foot of the Himalayas. The main exile temple of the fourteenth Dalai Lama, his private residence and a Tibetan Buddhist monastery have been there, at the far end of the McLeodganj area, for almost half a century. From 1 to 3 July, at the request of a group of Vietnamese Buddhists, a teaching event titled 'The Three Main Aspects of the Path' was to be held there.

During the three-day course, the Dalai Lama would begin by reading, explaining and commenting on the teachings medieval Buddhist master Je Tsongkhapa*.

On the morning of the last day, a special 'Medicine Buddha Ceremony' was to be held as part of the programme. The event took place in the heart of the multi-storey temple complex. This consisted of a large temple hall lined with pillars and a circular path lined with prayer wheels leading around the hall. It had windows and double doors on three of the four sides, adding brightness to the room.

At its head was a throne covered in colourful brocade. A larger-than-life golden Buddha statue could be seen towering behind it. Although the floor around the room is covered, the room is open on all sides. The 'living pillars' were creating a very special atmosphere. These were trees left to grow through holes in the floor and ceiling rather than being felled during construction work.

Countless people of different nationalities gathered to await the arrival of His Holiness. There were several Buddhist monks and nuns amongst them, not always easy to distinguish as they were all dressed in dark red robes and had shaved heads.

The majority of those waiting included both young and old Tibetans. Almost all the women wore the traditional *chupa*, a sleeveless, floor-length dress combined with a thin blouse and striped apron. With their thick black hair pinned up, the women looked very elegant, especially next to the Western tourists, who were dressed more casually in fluffy cotton trousers and worn-out T-shirts.

It was just eight in the morning, but more and more people started streaming into the complex, circling the Dalai Lama temple, praying, chatting and looking for a place on the floor to sit. A young Tibetan man stopped in front of the room, folded his hands in front of the large statue of the Buddha, and raised his folded hands high above his head. He then lowered his hands, still folded, first to his face and then to his chest. Then he threw himself flat on the ground with his palms facing forward. He repeated this ritual three times. Many Tibetans, young and old, nuns and monks, followed his example. In simple terms, he explained, believers use that gesture to express their respect for the 'Three Jewels' ('The Buddha', 'The Teaching' and 'The Community of Awakened Ones') of Buddhism. This form of physical exertion is also a good way of ridding oneself of the ignorance and illusion that says that Buddhism clouds the human mind.

The interior of Tsuklakhang Temple resembled a giant beehive. The babble of voices from the myriad mumbling and chattering guests mingled with the chanting of words blaring from loudspeakers. It was almost half past eight and the Dalai Lama was expected to arrive in a few minutes. With thousands of people in attendance, the air was heavy. Although there was nowhere to sit, they continued to stream into the temple complex. Most of them simply stood in the aisle, much to the annoyance of those seated. They had come with the hope of being able to catch at least one glimpse of His Holiness before the teachings began, or being greeted by his smile, or shaking his hand and exchanging a few words with him.

He plays a very central role in the lives of his fellow Tibetans even though the days when he had absolute religious and political power over his people are long gone and Tibetans in exile have a democratically elected parliament and His Holiness officially retired from all political office in 2011. Despite this, the enthusiasm, reverence and loyalty for the old monk, not only as a spiritual leader but also as the head of an entire nation, is immense.

As a representative of Tibetan culture and traditions, the fourteenth Dalai Lama has become an important figure of identification, especially for the 150,000 or so Tibetans living in exile around the world. As a result, many of his compatriots at the event brought traditional white khatas, which they gradually started taking out of their pockets and unfolded.

They knelt along the path the Dalai Lama was about to walk on, presenting the silken cloth as if it were an offering.

A grey-clad security guard mumbled into his walkie-talkie and signalled his colleague. The latter responded by energetically pushing the still-growing crowd of worshippers and curious onlookers behind a grey cordon. The atmosphere was becoming tense. The soft murmur of Vietnamese words from the loudspeaker stopped, and moments later, a deep male voice could be heard reciting the 'Mantra of Compassion'. *'Om mani padme hum,'* he repeated over and over again, in a catchy rhythm. Gradually, hundreds of devotees joined in the chanting. Eyes humbly fixed on the ground, hands raised, they waited in unison for their spiritual leader. It was a strange sensation—as if one had to hold one's breath, as if the quiet sound of air flowing from the mouth and nose were incongruous with the beauty and dignity of the sublime moment.

Led by a few incense-waving Tibetan monks, a five-man delegation of Vietnamese guests of honour and three bodyguards, the Dalai Lama walked along the path prepared for him. He wore a bright yellow-coloured scarf over his simple red-coloured monk's robe, and his feet were clad in red socks and simple brown leather shoes. Smiling mischievously but warmly, he raised his right hand to greet those kneeling before him. Despite the warning glances of his bodyguards, he took out plenty of time for his many followers. He acknowledged them all by glancing at them and, with a quick touch, blessed the handkerchiefs offered to him.

Wherever he went, he left a trail of happy faces. Just before entering the temple room, he paused one last time. He grasped the raised hands of an old Tibetan man and looked him straight in the eye. The two men exchanged a few words and smiled. Then the Dalai Lama turned and disappeared into the temple.

For a brief moment, everyone remained in a stupor as a result of His Holiness's appearance before them. Then, suddenly, the spell seemed to break. It felt like being able to breathe once again after a long, surreal dive. The barrier tapes were removed, and the streams of people began to move. Many of those present put on headphones to listen to the English translation of the lecture. Some took out pens and notepads, others closed their eyes and tried to absorb the atmosphere around them.

Meanwhile, the Dalai Lama took his seat on the golden throne in front of the richly decorated statue of the Buddha and started his lecture on Je Tsongkhapa's teachings, titled 'The Three Principal Aspects of the Path'. Tsongkhapa was a major Tibetan Buddhist teacher of the late fourteenth and early fifteenth centuries. He is regarded as the founder of the Gelug tradition, of which the Dalai Lama is the current head. The word 'path' in the title of his work refers to the path to enlightenment, which Buddhists aspire to attain.

By explaining and commenting on the teachings of the ancient masters, the Dalai Lama tried to give his listeners practical tips on how to follow the path to enlightenment more successfully. To this end, he talked about the following ritual repeatedly: first, he read a passage from Tsongkhapa's original Tibetan work of fourteen four-line sayings of wisdom. This was followed by a brief historical explanation and then His Holiness's personal interpretation of the words he had read. A Vietnamese nun, seated on the floor to the Dalai Lama's left, was translating everything that was being said. While the 300 or so Vietnamese guests of honour were able to enjoy an easily understandable translation, the rest of the guests had to make do with a noisy radio broadcast.

To truly understand Je Tsongkhapa's three fundamental aspects of the path to enlightenment, a sound knowledge of the

Buddhist concepts of 'causality', 'samsara' and 'enlightenment' is required. The content is, therefore, of particular interest to nuns, monks and others who actively practise Buddhism. However, listeners who are less familiar with the philosophy and interested non-Buddhists were also likely to find crucial takeaways from the talk. As in all his teachings, the Dalai Lama talked a lot about human values such as compassion, forgiveness and tolerance. He explained that these are 'cross-cultural and cross-religious', as people all around are equally striving for happiness and want to avoid suffering.

The Dalai Lama also emphasised at the beginning of his talk that Buddhism should not claim to be the best or the only true religion. Faith, he said, was something very personal. After all, neither is there a cure equally effective for all diseases and patients nor should we assume that there is a universal religion or philosophy that is right for everyone.

As he spoke, the Dalai Lama, sitting cross-legged in front of his audience, slowly started swaying his upper body from side to side. His voice reflected wisdom and his face looked relaxed. His eyebrows bobbed up and down as he spoke, and he constantly gestured with his right hand to emphasise his words.

Despite the calm and dignity that his whole demeanour exuded, it sometimes seemed as if he couldn't really stand still.

Unlike in the early morning, the lively atmosphere of the temple soon gave way to calm. After the butter tea, served by young monks from tiny pots, had been consumed and the sweet rolls distributed to everyone had been eaten, the audience started finding it noticeably harder to concentrate on the highly philosophical words of His Holiness.

On one hand, many children could be seen running around energetically, while on the other, some of the older visitors had already fallen asleep. Many of the Western visitors also seemed to be lost. By then, most of them had given up the battle with the mini-radio. Ironically, the model of the equipment was a product of the People's Republic of China—it was proving to be inadequate for receiving simultaneous English translations.

Shortly after half past eleven, a murmur suddenly rippled through the crowd. The Vietnamese nun, dressed in a lemon-yellow dress, had just finished her translation.

'*Tuk che nang*—Thank you,' said the Dalai Lama and began to clap. A few dozen Vietnamese guests joined in, creating a collective burst of energy in the ranks of the teaching visitors. His Holiness announced the end of the day's event and concluded it by telling a joke in a chuckling voice—but unfortunately in Tibetan.

By the time the Dalai Lama finally stepped down from his throne and prepared to leave the temple hall, most people had smiles on their faces; they seemed to be wide awake now. Rustling, whispering and murmuring could be heard from every corner.

As in the morning, young and old gathered along the path that led from the heart of the main temple to the exit. Once again, countless blessing scarves and folded hands were extended towards the monk. As before, he took out time to greet his people with a smile and a raised hand before slowly descending the stairs leading to his residence.

Shortly afterwards, thousands of visitors from all over the world poured into the streets of McLeodganj, after coming out from the great Tsuklakhang Temple complex.

The yellow walls glowed even brighter in the midday sun. But now that the teaching was over, the complex seemed eerily quiet. The gentle clatter of the pots and pans from the kitchen was the only sound one could hear, just like in the morning. It almost seemed as if everything that had happened there in the last few hours was an everyday occurrence.

An old woman walked around the corner, leaning on a wooden walking stick in her right hand, her left hand dangling. Slowly, but purposefully, she approached the exit. Her thin, old lips were curled in a quiet, unusual smile.

20

Opening of Home Josef 2

Soon, I travelled to the Himalayas with my friends again, this time for a very special event. It was the opening of our orphanage, Home Josef 2, in the Upper TCV, about 5 kilometres above the residence of His Holiness the Dalai Lama.

The construction of the home for about fifty Tibetan boys had taken more than two years as a result of heavy monsoon rains and snowfall in winter.

I had visited the site of the house, situated on a steep slope above McLeodganj, on several occasions. I was always impressed by the dedication with which the house was being built in such primitive conditions.

The most important thing was the foundation, which had been dug by hand with picks and shovels. That is how the local construction workers had performed their tasks for centuries. The walls of the foundations of the many houses for Tibetan refugee children, co-financed by sponsors from around the world, cling to the Himalayan foothills like swallows' nests.

Firmly anchored to withstand cold and heat, my Home Josef 2 would cater to future generations as well.

Weeks of torrential monsoon rains had affected the pillars, which were anchored in the rock using lots of expensive concrete and iron. Cement and sand had to be carried up on poles and painstakingly mixed with shovels on the few flat areas to form stable concrete. A separate group carried this sticky mixture in tin bowls down the steep slopes to the foundations, where it was then carefully mixed with plenty of iron to provide the necessary stability that would last centuries.

Countless staircases now connect the multi-storey building to the spacious attic, which serves as a meeting place for the fifty or so boys. School uniforms could be seen hanging on clotheslines, and rows of blue-painted wooden armchairs bore witness to the regular gatherings of the young residents after a busy school day. The work was finally finished!

Yes, it was my second home for the Tibetan children who had to flee over the snowy mountains. It was a small contribution to make their stay in exile in India—all the while learning about their own culture and traditions in close proximity to their religious and spiritual leader—a little easier. It was my contribution to the preservation of a thousand-year-old culture that is being sacrificed and destroyed by the power-holding entities of this world for the sake of economic greed and military might.

Late in the evening, before the scheduled opening, we sat on the terrace of our small hotel. The outlines and snowfields of the nearby 6,000-metre-high peaks, glistening in the moonlight, stood out against the dark blue night sky similar to something out of a picture book. Anyone could understand what was meant by the Milky Way by looking at the sky. Millions of stars formed a starry road in the clear sky.

The day before the opening of our second orphanage, we got down to enjoying our surroundings in our typical European way. I always advise my travelling friends to take some rubbing alcohol with them as a little germicide, so to speak. After handling it carefully all the way to the opening of our Tibetan orphanage, a friend had an idea for a special shooting-star game. We had a bottle of whisky and a bottle of cognac in our luggage. As per his plan, every time one of us spotted a shooting star in the Milky Way, which was adorned with millions of stars, we would have to finish our glass of 'ex'. It was no sooner said than done. After a short time, roughly after the twenty-third shooting star, we had to go back to our room, slightly drunk. We slept particularly well this time, and nobody dared to look out of the window at the Himalayan night sky.

The opening of our orphanage was scheduled for ten o'clock in the morning. For once, I had got up very early. It was pouring outside, and it made me more nervous than ever. This ceremony was not going to be like the one we had four years ago for our first Home Josef, when the celebrations were held beneath clear blue skies. All these thoughts were running through my head as I brushed my teeth. A small party had been planned for the opening this time. Only the children from the new Home Josef 2 and a few monks were to come. Mr Tsewang Jeshe, the director of all the orphanages in India, which housed some 18,000 Tibetan refugee children, had also agreed to come. Several mothers from neighbouring orphanages, along with Jakob and Felicitas, the Austrian couple who stayed in the area for almost thirty years, were also invited.

Tuktuk taxis took us to the nearby SOS Children's Village. Tsewang Jeshe, the director, and Lobsang Tsomo, the secretary, were waiting for us with open umbrellas. Together we walked the last few metres to the newly built orphanage. I had given them 300 Josef balloons the day before and they had decorated the whole building with them!

The fifty or so proud new residents welcomed us. They came from all parts of Tibet and were between twelve and fourteen years of age. Dressed in their-blue-and-white school uniforms, they stood in front of the narrow entrance to the house.

I briefly reviewed the years leading up to the completion of the three-storey building, which was financed by us. It had been difficult to build the orphanage on the steep hillside. The site was previously occupied by an old, dilapidated corrugated iron hut that was in constant danger of sliding down the slope.

Although there are three dormitories, sometimes three to four children have to sleep on a bunk bed designed for two—it tends to get quite crowded. Each dormitory has a shower and a Tibetan squat toilet. On the second floor, there is a dining room and lounge, a kitchen and a small storage room. The Tibetan housemother, who looks after the boys, also has a small room to herself. At the time of the opening ceremony, the house did not have a roof and was used as a place to wash, dry and play. We, of course, had plans in place to remedy this shortcoming and fund the necessary tin roof.

We leisurely walked past the rows of young Tibetans, all smiling happily at us. A black stone plaque had been placed at the entrance. The name of the orphanage was carved in huge letters: 'Home Josef 2'. Below, we could see the names of the main sponsors. Without them and the many small and large donations, the project would not have been possible. A well-known golf professor from Bad Ischl had organised a tournament for us and donated the relatively high proceeds to our cause. My Kiwanis friends, our payroll accountant from Innsbruck, a large tax consultancy from Linz, and also individuals such as Herby from Vienna—who donated a large sum on his sixtieth birthday—and not to forget the large sum raised by organising an annual charity event that I finance helped us realise the project.

Names of all these people were mentioned on the plaque at the entrance to Home Josef 2. It is very close to other orphanages, such as Haus Luxemburg or Haus RTL, and Maria Blumencron, the famous film director, provides for her sponsored children in a neighbouring house. We all felt very proud of our contribution and of our Home Josef 2.

Monks were also present at the opening ceremony. Tsewang Jeshe had earlier apologised to me for not being able to help me get an audience with the Dalai Lama. Unfortunately, he didn't have the time to meet us personally before. It was a shame, but we certainly understood his decision: he had to prioritise the many overseas trips, visits from high-ranking lamas, politicians and film stars.

However, we received a special gift from the Dalai Lama—he sent his most senior lama to the opening of our orphanage with special greetings. It was a great honour for us. The highest priest of his temple, Thamthog Rinpoche, would perform the inauguration! What a wonderful feeling—I almost wanted to bow down to express my gratitude, like the way Tibetan children and locals did.

First, Tsewang Jeshe gave a short speech and repeated his promise to help us get an audience with the Dalai Lama on my next visit.

Then the monks began the opening ceremony. In deep, gurgling voices, they chanted the mantras, while repeatedly throwing grains of wheat and rice into the air to symbolise the prosperity we were all praying for. None of us had ever witnessed such a ceremony before. We were deeply impressed.

At the very end, a tall Tibetan boy came forward and gave a speech in exemplary English. He politely thanked the monks and the people who had gathered at the ceremony. Then we listened to him talk about how most of his fellow villagers had come from distant Ladakh, situated on the border with China, while others had come from hopelessly overcrowded SOS Children's Villages in southern India. It was a heart-wrenching speech, coming from a man who had travelled all the way across the vast snowy mountains himself, and it left its mark on even my most hardened friends.

Next, it was my turn. A moment I had dreaded. I was the big sponsor, the Tibet activist, a rich and educated European in the eyes of these people. Unfortunately, I didn't speak English nearly as well as those Tibetan boys. Fortunately, Wangdoo, one of the Tibetan teachers, offered to translate my rather short thank-you speech word by word for the locals to comprehend. This gave me plenty of time to think about my choice of words and their correct pronunciation.

Monika, my wife, was sitting next to a very handsome and friendly boy of about fourteen during the entire ceremony. I felt bothered watching her talk to him the whole time. Later, she whispered in my ear: 'This poor boy still doesn't have a godmother! What do you think? Shouldn't I sponsor him?'

Sponsoring a Tibetan child is a task that takes years and is not always easy. It is by no means as simple as transferring the usual forty euros per month to the SOS Children's Village. It is much more important to stay in contact with the child, to share experiences, to visit them once a year and spend a few days with them, maybe even go on a holiday with them— and, most importantly, be their parent. But above all, it is about helping them shape their future. It's not an easy task, but it brings with it a feeling that can't really be described!

Monika, being aware of the challenges that would come her way, adopted Sonam as a godchild. My wife's godchild is currently studying mathematics and economics in South India. They exchange regular emails in which Sonam gives updates on his studies at the university. We feel happy seeing his progress. Just like real parents, we stand by him as he takes new steps in his life and support him as a family. Today, we are very proud of him and the fact that he is already employed as a manager at the Tibetan medical monastery Men-Tsee-Khang.

The opening ceremony marked the completion of our goal of building a second orphanage for Tibetan refugee children. But the best part of the project was the journey to get there, as I made many new friends along the way. Today, I daresay it was another big step towards getting closer to my second home.

Who else can say that? Yes, Monika is right in saying that it's a great feeling to have done something good!

Later, I talked to Tsewang Jeshe about my next project. I wanted to build a retirement home for Tibetan nomads. Coming from the vast Tibetan highlands, these mostly very old people settled in Ladakh after the Chinese military closed the borders. They have nothing and are the poorest of the poor. I wished to build a secure old age home for them.

In order to finance the cost of over 100,000 euros, we shared the project with the city of Bolzano and the Austrian organisation, Save Tibet. The old age home on the border with China was opened just three years later.

Built at an altitude of around 4,500 metres, the home can accommodate more than a hundred mountain nomads. Due to time constraints, I was unable to attend the opening ceremony. But a year later, when I visited the home with two friends, I was richly rewarded. It was a wonderful feeling. We were not greeted by playing children or friendly boys; instead, we saw old people limping out of the six big residential buildings. They tried to greet us with a friendly smile on their mostly toothless faces.

It was not the lack of time for care or the need for both parents to work, as in Europe, that became the reason behind deciding to build old people's homes in the mountainous highlands. It was for the old and frail who were forced to cross the border with their huge herds of yaks, goats or sheep, often at night on secret routes, because of the heavily guarded border with China and Pakistan, in order to use the few fertile valleys for their livestock. The old men and women thus became a burden on their families. Because of them, the young ones couldn't move quickly enough to find good grazing lands for their herds.

For generations, these families have been the rulers of the vast, barren steppes of the Tibetan highlands. Today, they are being driven from their homeland, driven away by a foreign military power that is greedy for natural resources and strategic military superiority. Often, the elders of the family have sneaked away from their loved ones, to wait in small makeshift dwellings for their imminent death.

But now that we have come up with our old age home in the border region of Ladakh, it should serve as a new refuge, a 'Home Josef 3' for these hitherto hopeless people! Another home of this kind might soon have to be built.

21

Meeting the God of Love

I could feel it. It was going to be a very special day full of unique experiences, becoming the climax of an extraordinary pilgrimage. It was probably the unimaginable power of a mysterious flow, a form of happy enthusiasm that could only be surpassed by the happiness of a mother giving birth! When such a flow is coupled with the melancholy of a seemingly unattainable love, it feels like an armada of butterflies visiting your heart. It was one of those rare moments in the life of an emotional, emphatic person. It was probably one of those seemingly unattainable, beautiful pains that cannot be described in lines.

My knees trembled, and I could feel beads of sweat on my forehead. The uncontrollable elemental force of my emotional world could sense that the day had arrived. An inner voice told me, as never before in my life, that it was the day to feel, a day when I could scream and cry with happiness. It said to me that I was now standing at the gate to my paradise, on my way to nirvana, like the last few metres to the summit of Mount Everest, where my long search for happiness had finally reached its destination.

The neurotic stamps of my Western homeland immediately showed their dominance and demanded resistance. They brought doubt into play, something like *'Wait and see, don't rejoice too soon, you're not there yet. Who knows what will happen next.'* The uncertainty surfaced like boiling lava and promptly retreated into some unknown place inside me. Too often, great happiness had collapsed despite coming so close to the finish line. *'Wait and see,'* said hope. It was becoming unbearable. I let out a scream as if Bruce Lee was about to deliver a final blow to the man with the death claw. Then I straightened up vigorously, lifted my chin and stretched out again. Then I picked up my things and finally made my way to the arranged meeting, my meeting with him.

Once again, I was a guest in my second home, India. I was again in McLeodganj, a small township near Dharamshala.

I was carrying the rough draft of my new, almost finished book in my rucksack. It still carried the working title 'Thank You Tibet', although I had already decided to crown it with the real reason for my travels. I was a traveller 'in search of happiness', and had planned on changing the title after returning home.

The moment of my personal transformation would be evident in my texts to any attentive reader of my work. Indeed, the book chronicles a journey spanning approximately twenty-five years, a minuscule moment in the vastness of our globe but a seemingly endless journey to me.

The locals were observing an anniversary. After fleeing their homeland of Tibet, the refugees had been given a piece of land in the inaccessible Himalayas by the former Indian prime minister Jawaharlal Nehru. But they had no reason to celebrate or dance for joy. The anniversary that day was not to mark a happy occasion. It was the sixtieth anniversary of the expulsion of these people from their homeland by soldiers of the Chinese army, after thousands of years of seclusion in the endless expanses of the snowy mountains.

I was just four years old when the Tibetans were forced into a cruel exodus. When I travel to visit my Tibetan friends, I feel their pain as if I were a part of them. Over the past twenty-five years of travelling to the most remote areas of Tibetan refugees, I have experienced the great hospitality of their families. I have made friends with high lamas, and studied and learned about their culture, beliefs and mysterious spiritual science through endless stories. Yes, it must be true—the reincarnation of the spirit, rebirth into an earthly being who, according to the stories of my Tibetan friends, is always seeking a new body for the infinite cycle of life repeatedly until, often after thousands of years, they find the infinite peace of nirvana, paradise in Buddhist heaven!

Every time I hear the deep sounds of the Tibetan monks or the shrill, high-pitched chanting of the Tibetan women, I feel deeply. My body speaks to me, *'You were once one of them.'* I feel happy hearing this inner voice. It is unbelievably peaceful and brings in a sense of security. I feel at home. It is the familiar feeling of having 'arrived home'.

Everything would have been fine had it not been for the controlling and regimented Western culture I was brought up in. I'm probably so dependent on it that it makes me feel insecure all the time and makes me doubt everything. I keep hearing their objections, related to Far Eastern charlatanism, mysterious fairy tales, and foreign incomprehensible cultures. Then there are many unanswered questions that worry me. We westerners are used to always looking for evidence for unanswered questions. I, on the other hand, have felt more and more often that there is something that my Western culture cannot answer with the dogma of its usual questions of 'how, why and what'! For more than two decades, I have been writing down the experiences and stories of my Tibetan friends, the moving tales of their escape across the Himalayas to the largest democratic country in the world, India. And yes, it took me a quarter of a century to finish this book, and I had to figure out several things on my own and in my own way. Looking back, I started on this journey over twenty-five years ago and it seems far from over. With time, I have come to realise that I am treading on the path of a Buddha. My love for charity made me build three orphanages. The hospitality of my Tibetan friends has taught me tolerance. Somehow, I could never really grasp the third great virtue of Buddhism: self-confidence. My respect and caution towards other cultures prevented it. However, while writing my book, I could feel a sense of self-confidence as I sat down to write about my experiences as a guest—and yes, maybe even as one of them. It took me more than twenty-five years of work and twenty-five years of friendship before I could simply go to His Holiness as one of the 3,000 visitors to attend his teachings, to pause for a moment despite a serious illness, and to crown my work with a photograph as a legacy for all who read this. I was probably one of the few people he had hugged, but more on that in the next few lines.

The lifelong efforts of Tibetans' living god, His Holiness the Dalai Lama, to be allowed to return to his Tibetan homeland have so far been in vain. The Western world has expressed understanding and sympathy, most notably by awarding the Nobel Peace Prize to this ever-cheerful monk for his unprecedented peaceful struggle. It didn't help. And how could it have worked? With China's ever-violent rulers, the battle of David against Goliath could never be won!

The Dalai Lama has a few paradigms. One is that if even one Tibetan were to kill another in the fight for freedom, he would resign as head of state and religious leader and end his life in the solitude of a monastery in the Tibetan mountains.

Unfortunately, he has to accept that Buddhist monks continue to sacrifice themselves by self-immolation to draw attention to the plight of Tibet's defenceless people. However, the kind of terrorist attacks we are familiar with in Europe do not occur in Tibet. Combined with the deep Buddhist belief in rebirth, the 'living Buddha' has been at least able to prevent such things with his clear words.

My book was supposed to be about these people. But then—almost sixty years after their exodus—I experienced the wave of European refugees. Like thousands of other Europeans, I did my bit to help displaced people from Syria, Afghanistan and other war zones around the world. Since then, I have been able to employ around twenty-five refugees at my host company. People from some seventeen different nationalities have been working hard to support my business in the equally tough economic struggle for survival in an Austrian gastronomic culture that is unfortunately threatened with extinction.

But I also learnt about the other side of the story regarding those people who ruthlessly abandon their families in war-torn regions. These are young people, full of strength and energy, who do not use their energy against the resistance, for peace, or to return to their homeland. These people, under the guise of 'refugees', shamelessly exploit the generosity of Europeans, the hard-won prosperity of a people who were also occupied not so long ago. These people try to destroy our culture and try to impose their beliefs on us by any means necessary—even including ruthless violence!

This was reason enough for me to refocus on the topic being talked about in my book and broaden its context. The stark contrast between the helpfulness and gratitude displayed by the Tibetan refugees—not to forget the countless 'good' and 'hard-working' refugees—and the criminal behaviour of some European refugees is obvious and, from my point of view, shows the often-abused way in which the generous European willingness to help is handled.

My greatest wish, of course, was to receive a foreword from His Holiness himself. When I asked the Dalai Lama's office, they initially wanted me to share my manuscript in advance. But as they couldn't read it in German, they ended up trusting my long-standing friendship with the Dalai Lama, who then supported my book in an uncomplicated way with a very touching foreword. The interaction helped me get an opportunity to disseminate their messages and the legacy of their culture. Two years of the pandemic and the many closures in India delayed the publication of my book. Once again, I realised how much I needed the calm and quiet of that period. I was able to utilise all that time to revise the manuscript.

I keep remembering the prophecy of a famous Tibetan lama from the eighth century: 'Only when birds of steel and carriages of iron invade Tibet will the spirit of the Tibetans spread throughout the world.'

The idea of looking for a tiny positive seed in every act, no matter how cruel, is a remarkable principle of Tibetan culture. Today, at last, the seed of their culture has spread throughout the world, and we are all benefiting from the legacy.

I attended His Holiness's rare teachings in Dharamshala, accompanied by a small group of Tibetan friends. Weeks before, the media had reported that the Dalai Lama was suffering from a serious lung condition. I happened to be in Delhi when his release from hospital was broadcast live on television.

When asked about his health, he jokingly replied that it was only a slight cold and it forced him to travel from the pleasant Himalayan mountains to the sweltering heat of Delhi.

I thankfully had the foresight to make a copy of the cover of my book, which was not yet ready for printing, so that I could take a photograph with him and my new book. I wanted to ask my Tibetan and Indian friends to support me for a short audience.

How foolish I was to think that His Holiness would take the time for a photo session with me and my book! In the run-up to the scheduled teaching, rumours were circulating that the Dalai Lama had fallen ill again and would not be able to attend.

But before I left for the Himalayas, I had asked my long-time friend, the Maharaja of Kangra, Aditya Katoch, in whose Himalayan kingdom the Tibetan government-in-exile is based, to put in a good word for my plans if any suitable opportunity arose. His wife, Chandresh Kumari, the sister of the Maharaja of Jodhpur, who had been minister for culture, women's rights and tourism for nearly forty-eight years, was campaigning for what would probably be her last election. I knew she was good friends with the Dalai Lama. Her grandson Ambikeshwar, the heir and heir apparent to one of the oldest families in the world, the Katoch dynasty of India, was granted permission to do his yearly internship in the Dalai Lama's office. So if anyone could help me, it was she!

I went to see His Holiness's secretary the evening before the teachings to clarify this possibility. Mr Chemi explained that many similar requests had already been cancelled due to

His Holiness's advancing illness, but I should wait outside His Holiness's office just before the teaching the next day. I was happy to know that at least my meeting had not been cancelled. My excitement at the possibility of meeting the Dalai Lama was gradually mixed with uncertainty and the question of whether I had been a little too overzealous in pushing for this meeting with him. But how could I not be impatient? I was, after all, going to be meeting His Holiness for the eighth time in the last ten years!

I have always felt an inner impulse to write down what my Tibetan friends have told me for over twenty years! I had written many of my stories sitting in the garden of the Dalai Lama Temple, exactly where the next day's teaching was to take place. I often wrote in a trance but kept on writing. It was the only way I could preserve the authenticity of my words.

By around eight o'clock the next morning, an endless queue of people had formed in front of the security checks at the temple. I knew that if I joined the queue, the meeting would never happen! So I took the khata, the welcome shawl, I had brought for His Holiness out of my bag, draped it around my neck and walked confidently past the thousands of monks and visitors!

I passed the security check with ease and waited calmly outside the secretary's office, with a pounding heart. Mr Chemi had just arrived for work. He greeted me warmly and asked one of the Tibetan security guards to join him. However, I wasn't entirely sure what he whispered in the local dialect. But it soon became clear. The guard, armed with a machine gun, suddenly came straight to me and demanded to see my book. I showed it to him, along with a copy of His Holiness's foreword. Somehow, he was satisfied with that and then escorted me through thousands of high Tibetan dignitaries and guests sitting on the floor and waiting for the teaching.

At the entrance, he asked me to wait. He took great pains to explain how many distinguished people had been refused an audience because of the Dalai Lama's serious illness.

Suddenly, the temple, which could hold about 3,000 people, fell silent. His Holiness, supported by several monks, struggled up the steps to the top temple of the huge monastery! He was followed by a retinue of high Buddhist dignitaries. He did not approach me or the visitors with his usual demeanour, with a smile on his face, as on previous occasions. He instead walked with heavy footsteps, hunched over, held up by his closest advisers.

This was not the ever-friendly monk, the living God-King. His Holiness had become a frail old monk. In front of me, I saw a man in pain, bloated with medication. This man in poor health, but a reincarnation of the Buddha, was trying with his last ounce of strength to meet the expectations of thousands of Buddhist pilgrims.

Meanwhile, the Dalai Lama was moving in my direction, so the secretary pushed me into the middle of the aisle, right in front of the oncoming crowd.

Watery, tired eyes looked lovingly at me. I knew he would recognise me! The entire entourage following him stopped. I bowed deeply, trying to hide my tears.

Mr Chemi explained to His Holiness why I wanted to meet him. The Dalai Lama took my hands, gave me a sideway hug, muttered something in Tibetan as a photographer took the picture I had hoped for. He hugged me tightly. I was unsure if I should get so close to his aura, but I let it happen. When he embraced me, I could no longer control my emotions. Finally, I had an emotional outburst as if a volcano had erupted, fuelled by an earthquake. I fought not to fall to my knees before him, to hold on to him as tears were streaming from my eyes and my whole body was shaking. The entourage of monks watched with tense faces.

The Dalai Lama sensed my emotion and looked deeply into my eyes. He said in a faint voice: 'Tibet needs friends, friends like you, Günter La. There is nothing more important. Carry the message of our people to the world, so that people out there can learn from us!'

When it was time to bid goodbye, he once again gave me a sideway hug, and I felt the soft, precious fabric of his clothes. Then he took his leave with an eager smile and the procession moved towards his golden throne in the temple.

As if in a trance, I walked backwards, stooping low and bowing, so as to not turn my back on His Holiness—as was done for ancient pilgrims of the Himalayan empire. Only the iron railing of the temple brought me back to reality, when I bumped into it most painfully. Then an uneasy feeling came over me—this wise monk, one of the great models of our humanity, would not be with us for long. Could this be one of my last encounters with him?

His Tibetan people, inclusive of the refugees, scattered around the world will continue to fight for their right to return to their homeland.

They will continue to tread on the Buddhist path and spread their culture in the world, all the while helping others. Tibetan refugees are very peaceful.

I couldn't stay to attend the teaching for long. My emotions were stirred as never before. I had never left a temple filled with thousands of pilgrims so quickly. I forgot about my group members, who were sitting among all the visitors, watching my hasty departure with questioning eyes. Tears of joy had driven away my gloomy thoughts and I walked alone and thoughtfully into the wide valley until a small café caught my attention. There I lit a cigar, ordered a double whisky and began to write with all the emotion of an absolutely happy man: 'Never give up, Your Holiness. This world still needs you, we have very few great examples like you!'

22

My Friend, the Maharaja

Hans-Jörg Hörtnagl was the Austrian trade delegate in Delhi. I had met him a long time ago in my pub in Linz. It was one of those rare encounters that marked the beginning of a friendship that would last years.

He was Tyrolean, but that was not the only reason why we liked each other right away. We both liked to drink good Austrian wine and talk about God and the world. I often told Hans-Jörg about my travels and Tibetan projects in northern India. He always listened with great interest and I had promised to visit him in Delhi on one of my next trips to India. No sooner said than done—we met regularly during my stopovers on my way to the Himalayas. This gave me many opportunities to make new acquaintances and contacts in his beautiful residence which was in an area in Delhi where most ambassadors lived.

It was during one such visit that I happened to meet Tempa Tsering, the husband of the Dalai Lama's sister and head of His Holiness's office in Delhi. From the outset, our sympathies were obviously mutual, and in the highly interesting conversations that ensued, he repeatedly gave me fascinating insights into the private world of his 'boss', the Dalai Lama. For example, his ritualised daily routine, which is always the same 'unless he is travelling', as Tsering pointed out. Early in the morning, at four o'clock on the dot, he gets out of bed and starts the day with tea prepared for him. Nothing unusual, of course, but who would have thought that the Dalai Lama would be so concerned about his fitness? So every morning, he gets on the old pedal bike in his small room in Dharamshala. This is not one of those high-tech ergometers that instantly calculate and prescribe the best rhythm for a successful workout. No, he wouldn't be the Dalai Lama if he didn't still use his old stationary bike for his fitness training, even though the 'thing' could probably be described as antique today. Afterwards, he devotes himself to extensive meditation before attending to the tasks of everyday life and the duties of his office. Only in the late afternoon would he indulge in a modest meal, as he did not eat in the evening. This 'harms the body', but Tsering leaves no doubt that the Dalai Lama always has the right answer when it comes to health.

Over the years, Tempa Tsering has been a reliable friend and helper on my travels. Time and again, he has put me in touch with important contacts in Dharamshala. The only thing he wasn't very happy about was my big plan for His Holiness to visit my hometown of Linz during his ten-day stay in Austria in 2012, because of Dalai Lama's busy schedule. However, as a kind of 'compensation', I received a personal invitation for an audience with the Dalai Lama during his major lecture at the Salzburgarena.

Our friendship has not been negatively impacted. A few weeks ago, I asked him for another favour. I had written an article for a friend's book. A photograph of me with the Dalai

Lama was to be included. He was happy to grant my request, and I received a positive email from the office of the Dalai Lama's secretary.

One of the most interesting contacts, however, was with the Maharaja of Kangra, Raja Aditya Katoch. I met him about fifteen years ago through Hans-Jörg. Since then, we have enjoyed a very special, almost brotherly friendship. Aditya can boast of being the head of one of the oldest traceable families in the world. Their traceable family tree dates to 4300 BC, a time long before the Egyptians started building their first pyramids. Even *Guinness World Records* has honoured his family with an entry.

I still remember how it all began. I had just arrived in Dharamshala when my mobile rang. It was Aditya on the phone. 'Hello Günter, how are you? You are a friend of Hans-Jörg, aren't you?' I answered in the affirmative and the strong voice continued: 'Would you like to join us for dinner? We are at Clouds & Villa—easy to find, just below the temple complex of His Holiness!'

I could hardly believe it. It was a dinner invitation from the Maharaja himself. Well, I was definitely up for it! But I didn't have much time. So, I hurriedly put on my cleanest hitch-hiker's trousers and took a taxi, which dropped me off right in front of the small villa complex. Everything was as described—about 300 metres above the 'modest' estate, you could see the thick walls of the temple complex and the Dalai Lama's residence. The two were practically neighbours.

To be on the safe side, I had looked up my unexpected host on his company's website. His palace, the Lambagraon, had been destroyed by an earthquake in 1905 and underwent renovation. He also owns a palace hotel in Rajasthan, an Indian state known as the 'kingdom of kings'. He also owns a lodge that can be reached in about two hours from Dharamshala. It is said to be a wonderful place for trout fishing. This rather small and simple guest house complex for a Maharaja consists of about a dozen not too grand villas. Richard Gere is said to have stayed in one of these.

Aditya's clan is still one of the impoverished families of the once incredibly wealthy maharajas. Deposed by the British and stripped of all his rights after the abolition of princely states in India, he was left with nothing but his title. His fate in India was similar to that of our own imperial dynasty of the Habsburgs—once incredibly powerful throughout Europe, now on the verge of oblivion. In both cases, their once magnificent palaces can only be preserved as cultural monuments with the help of the state, although it should be remembered that the state has largely expropriated the Habsburgs' property and, as the owner, has to pay for its upkeep anyway.

In the taxi, I phoned Hans-Jörg to thank him again for putting me in touch with him. In passing, I learned that Aditya and his wife had been on a state visit to Vienna a few weeks earlier—his wife had recently been appointed India's minister of culture.

Now I felt a bit self-conscious. I was wearing my hitchhiking trousers, a T-shirt that wasn't quite clean, and sandals. I had only winter clothes in my luggage—my hitchhiking gear for the mountains and jeans, slightly torn, as was the current fashion in trendy bars in Europe. But I couldn't attend the invitation in such an attire.

The taxi had pulled up through a small, shady forest of Himalayan cypresses. The coat of arms of the 'rajas of Lambagraon' was emblazoned at the entrance. Awe-struck, I climbed the stairs, which were already a little damaged by the rainfall, and called out 'Hello', hesitantly at first, then a little louder. The dogs began to bark, and an Indian servant came towards me. He greeted me with 'Namaste', then escorted me into a rather low anteroom of this already rather unadorned complex. They poured me tea, served me biscuits, and left me alone.

I examined the tastefully decorated room carefully. I wanted to remember as many details as possible. Huge paintings hung on the walls, all depicting magnificently dressed, bearded maharajas. I had no doubt that these were Aditya's ancestors. Behind my sofa hung the huge skin of a tiger, its mouth wide open. I was about to snap a quick photo when Raja Aditya Katoch of the legendary Katoch family appeared. He was quite tall and had to bend forward slightly to get through the small door into the room.

This man exuded a great aura. The few white hairs slicked back tightly, and the typical long white Indian clothes made him look even taller. There was no doubt that this man was of royal blood.

As a precaution, I had brought a bottle of blue gin from my friend, the famous Austrian distiller Reisetbauer, which I presented to him as a gift. He smiled: 'How's Hans-Jörg?'

I introduced myself and bowed slightly. He asked me to sit down. 'Whisky or gin?' he asked me, and I decided on whisky. There I was, sitting next to a real raja. His family had been one of the most powerful on this continent for thousands of years. From a book he proudly presented to me, I learned that it was his ancestors who turned back Alexander the Great and his invincible warriors in the lowlands of the Kangra Valley.

There are still many stories about these people, who were also known as 'the golden-skinned people'. I remember travelling through Kinnaur, a region situated just before Spiti on the border with Tibet. From my window, I saw a beautiful, tall woman with long hair, slender fingers and pale blue eyes—an unusual sight in the Himalayas—playing lovingly with her children. She soon realised that I was there, but she didn't show it. Instead, she continued to glance at me slyly until she eventually gave me a cautious smile. She must have belonged to that mysterious race of Alexander's warriors. Their descendants are said to live in the region to this day, and she must have been one of them.

Fortunately, Aditya hadn't noticed that I was lost in thought, and continued to leaf through his huge book. He was visibly proud and tried his best to explain its significance to me. Then he showed me the photograph of the huge palace of the Maharaja of Jodhpur. I had never seen anything like it—so magnificent. This palace was only slightly smaller than Buckingham Palace because the British had forbidden it to be surpassed in size. They had smilingly bowed to this prohibition and then simply left out a 'few metres'. Aditya had good reason to be proud of this palace. He was, after all, married to the sister of the maharaja of Jodhpur and thus a member of the famous family himself.

Despite all this, Aditya remained a modest and simple man. He clearly enjoyed entertaining guests at his summer residence and proudly told me that the Danish ambassador would be visiting next weekend.

I was deeply impressed, but I didn't know then that I would soon have the honour of meeting many other important people through him.

Once again, I thought of our mayor in Linz. I had never been invited to his office, although it is very close to my restaurant. Like Don Camillo and Peppone, we have been fighting for about twenty years. I simply never agreed with the way he treated us restaurateurs in Linz. After all, we were the city's hosts, but every time he had a chance, he would get a fellow restaurateur beaten up by his officials. I smiled a little in my mind—here I was sitting with the Maharaja of Kangra, and not so long ago, he was one of the most powerful people on the Indian subcontinent.

And just a few hundred metres away was Aditya's neighbour, the Dalai Lama, who at his last meeting with about 3,000 people had pointed at me, smiled and said: 'I know you, I remember you.' On learning that he remembered me despite meeting countless people almost every day, I felt a little proud of myself.

Now, I was seated with a glass of expensive whisky, in the company of a maharaja whose former kingdoms are said to have stretched from Afghanistan through Pakistan to the gates of Delhi. It was sheer amazement for me—and it was about to get even better.

The maharaja pointed his finger at a painting depicting an imposing fortress. This was the legendary Kangra Fort. Built on a huge rock, it was framed by steep ravines that ended in a wide, deep river. It was the family seat of the rajas of Kangra, Aditya's family.

Long before the European dynasties of knights built their impregnable castles in Scotland or England, this fortress stood as a visible model for knights in our latitudes, the Maharaja proudly mentioned. Only the cannons of the British and the great earthquake of 1905 were able to topple this impregnable fortress. Today, attempts are being made to rebuild the landmark, which can be seen from afar.

'Would you like to see the castle? If you want to, I can take you there tomorrow!' Aditya's question came out of the blue—but sounding as if it was the most normal thing in the world to ask. I was speechless for a few seconds—of course I wanted to go!

We had both finished half a bottle of whisky and were a bit drunk. I said goodbye, still excited, and promised to be back in time for our trip the next day. Of course, I was back at the villa on time at two in the afternoon. Aditya was waiting in his small but very capable off-road jeep and off we went, together on the long journey up the Kangra Valley to the legendary Kangra Fort.

A maharaja for a chauffeur—I thought I would go mad! During the drive, he explained the area to me in dazzling words and gestures. The snow-capped mountains of the Himalayas glittered behind us, and we drove past seemingly endless rice terraces. The Kangra Valley is rightly regarded as one of the most fertile regions in India.

The mighty remains of Kangra Fort were visible from afar. Unfortunately, it was incredibly hot and I began to understand why all the people fled to the cooler mountains. Aditya stopped in front of a building with huge battlements, still a long way from our destination. We were now to visit the family museum that Aditya had set up in this venerable building.

As we got out, the visitors to the museum recognised the Maharaja. It was then that I realised once again what a great honour it was for me to be in his company. Most of the guests bowed deeply to him and some even honoured him by touching his feet and then kissing his hands. Aditya grinned and obviously enjoyed it.

The tour that followed was even more interesting than I had expected. The Maharaja opened all the cupboards and showcases, and behind those we could see the treasures that were kept there. Cupboards with fine crockery, antique weapons, magnificent glassware from Venice were only a few of the several items that caught my attention. I wanted to take good photographs.

The presence of several security cameras confirmed the value of these treasures. Aditya showed me writings by his ancestors, the ornate sleigh that stood in the middle of the covered courtyard, mannequins in sumptuous robes and a beautiful four-poster bed. Everything was incredible. The walls were densely hung with mostly huge paintings of his ancestors. There was a simple photograph that stood out: it was of the Dalai Lama, with Aditya and his wife, the princess of Jodhpur, and their son. They had all been guests in this house not a long time ago.

What an honour for me, a small landlord from Austria! My connection with Hans-Jörg, his network, and the great hospitality of the Maharaja had made everything possible. I was really proud and satisfied!

We bid adieu to the guards and made the long journey back. On the way, Aditya invited me as his guest the next day. The secretary to the former home minister and foreign minister of India as well as a famous actor from Delhi and the head of government of Dharamshala were also in the guest list. What an honour!

Aditya dropped me off with Nick outside my modest guest house. I thanked him and promised to bring him a very special bottle of Austrian wine the following day.

I lay in bed for a long time, letting the memories of the day pass by. It was such a gift. I had long since cancelled my plans to continue on to Spiti. The fact that the pass was not yet open made my decision easier.

Since my visit the previous year, I had been trying to write down about my many experiences in the Himalayas. I spent every spare minute sitting on Nick's terrace, jotting down everything I could recollect, for a possible book.

Every day, I would fight for a particular table on the terrace, as it was close to the lone electrical socket. My laptop's battery lasted only a few hours and that was never enough to record my many impressions and memories in front of Nick's café, which had a wonderful view of the Kangra Valley.

Armed with a camera and a bottle of my favourite wine, I arrived for dinner at the Maharaja's on time. The bottle of 'Salzberg 2007' from my favourite winemaker Gernot Heinrich, which I had taken with me for very special occasions, was my gift to the host. I was convinced that Gernot would be delighted to hear which celebrities enjoyed his rare and precious red wine.

Aditya's guests had arrived before me. The Maharaja introduced them to me one by one. Unfortunately, I couldn't remember all their names. So I diligently handed out my business cards and always got a few in return. Now, I had to be careful in giving them to the right people. It was funny when the foreign secretary asked me what the title under my name meant: I had written 'landlord' as my job title on the card. No doctor, no minister, no academic degree, just host, just landlord.

We sat down and had another good whisky as an aperitif. I tried to understand some of the conversation of those present. They were talking about high politics, about the pervasive corruption, about how difficult it was to reconcile thousands of cultures and hundreds of different languages in India. But the political situation with China was a recurring theme. None of them were great friends with their communist neighbour. Of particular importance were my many audiences with His Holiness. All of them were very fond of the Dalai Lama and his people, as they had repeatedly pointed out.

I picked up on a very interesting story told by the Secretary to the Minister of Home Affairs: During a conversation with the Dalai Lama, the latter told him that he had received an urgent late night phone call from Beijing. The person on the other end was the daughter of a senior Chinese political figure. She earnestly asked him to pray for her sick father, so that he might recover. Months later, during another visit, the minister asked the Dalai Lama about the call from Beijing. His Holiness reported that he and his monks had been praying for the woman's father for fourteen days. He was now doing well.

A few days later, I read an article in an Indian newspaper specifying that the said Chinese state minister was one of the very few politicians who belonged to the Buddhist faith. I had to smile—what strange connections.

The bottle of Salzberg was opened and poured into a glass jug to give the precious wine some air. Then we toasted to a special evening. As far as I could find out, the guests, all of whom were friends with one another, met in Dharamshala every year whenever they wished to escape the summer heat in Delhi. Once again, I had the unbelievable good fortune of being in the right place at the right time.

I spent many more wonderful days with Aditya. I made friends with many in his high-profile circles. Today, more than twenty-five years later, I realise how much my acquaintance with Aditya and his stories, most of which have been passed down through generations, have influenced me. If I may quote an old unwritten law: 'Nothing in life happens without a reason.' Believing in the same, I count myself as the chosen one who has the task of listening and writing down all these stories, tales and experiences. I always doubted whether all of that would fit into one. So much has happened...

It was around midnight when I was driven to Nick's by the Home Secretary's driver, who was visibly drunk. It was the end of a day that had passed like a dream.

23

St John in the Wilderness

Just ten minutes' walk from McLeodganj, in a vast cedar forest, is the Anglican Church of St John in the Wilderness. This rather bare and unadorned place of worship is romantically nestled in a small clearing surrounded by one of the most beautiful cemeteries in the world. It is both mystical and charming, especially when the mist rises from the Kangra Valley in the morning, revealing the golden roofs of the Dalai Lama's temple on a hill above Dharamshala. Around the church, there are several graves, both old and new, often carelessly marked with stones collected in a rush.

I take out time from each of my many visits to McLeodganj to stroll through the deserted cemetery, close to the grazing cows. Strange thoughts keep running through my head: the bodies of the former British colonial rulers now fertilise the grass of the sacred cows; what moving stories the people buried there, mostly soldiers of the British occupation forces, have to tell, far from their European homeland ...

Only the 3-metre-high, somewhat weathered but still impressive artistic monument to the British Governor General and viceroy of India, Lord Elgin*, bears witness to the site's centuries-old British past. A military unit of the British colonial power was stationed there long before the Tibetans settled there.

Barely legible brass plaques on the walls of the church tell of the Englishmen who died in the service of their country and were buried at the site. The plaques also tell the stories of individuals, as evidenced by the many 'last greetings' from distant family members. On one I read the story of a brave Englishman who was killed by a bear in the Himalayas.

A holy mass is held there every Sunday, giving the few Christians a chance to worship together. I have attended these services on several occasions. An Indian priest celebrates the mass, and only a few local believers are present. These are mostly dropouts, and tourists who come here to find the peace and quiet they are looking for, along with a link to the faith of their European homeland. As you enter the church, which is built from massive Himalayan boulders, you notice the many signboards imposing restrictions. These are clearly purely European rules: 'No photo', 'No dogs', 'Please be quiet', 'No smoking'. But what's the point? They are decidedly inappropriate. They contradict the openness and tolerance of Buddhist freedom. The signboards made me angry and immediately reminded me of my over-regulated homeland of Austria. One will never find such signboards in a Tibetan monastery or a Hindu temple. The respect and ethics of the people in the mountains alone ensure that they always behave respectfully and attentively in such 'houses of silence'.

Alexandra, a long-time Dutch friend, went to Goa in the days of the hippies and flower children. The Indian way of life made such a deep impression on her that since then she has only left the country for important family occasions. Alexandra has now lived in India for over forty years. She earns a modest living by giving courses in Tibetan medicine, or by organising festivals, and using the social shadow of our mutual friend, the Maharaja of Kangra, Aditya Katoch. He supports her which helps her sustain with a slightly higher standard of living.

Alexandra has been my true angel in India. No matter what I need, no matter what I want to know, Alexandra knows and organises everything, be it a vehicle for a tour or medicine for friends back home. Because I always want to know exactly what I need, she often explains the customs and cultures of the locals, especially the ones that I don't understand. She is the one who has told me countless stories and myths about my legendary friend, the Maharaja, and his family traditions of more than 4,000 years. Fortunately, she speaks good German, English of course, and a little Hindi. She even understands the complicated Tibetan language quite well, although she doesn't speak it herself.

On my last visit, we sat on the little bench in front of St John in the Wilderness Church and talked about death. What an unconventional subject! In our part of the world, people usually only talk about death when someone is being buried. Unfortunately, the focus is often on inheritance issues and the negative deeds of the deceased. Relatives mourn, cry and usually remember the positive aspects of a lost friend or relative far too late.

For a Tibetan, however, the path of rebirth or reincarnation is a lifelong process that begins at birth. All of a person's deeds, both positive and negative, influence the life in which they reincarnate after death. The wheel of life, or dharma, continues to turn until a person reaches nirvana, which is equivalent to our heavenly paradise and is the ultimate goal pursued by all Buddhists. The Buddhist mantra *'om mani padme hum'*, every turn of a prayer wheel, every circumambulation of a temple, a stupa or a pile of mani stones, whether small or big, helps to get closer to the goal—always thinking and striving to be born in a better world after death.

For many westerners, it may be only now that they have come to understand why Tibetans are mostly vegetarians. There are reborn energies in all living beings. Killing them, mistreating them, torturing them or instilling negative energy in them would result in a worse rebirth, regardless of whether the being in question is a worm or a human. If only we could incorporate a little of this loving kindness and mindfulness into our way of life! People all over the world would be able to coexist a bit peacefully if we were a little more committed to this philosophy. After all, tolerance and love for our neighbour are not simply propagated by Buddhism alone—these concepts are accepted by all religions of the world.

Alexandra had a booklet on her lap and was flipping through it, feeling a little embarrassed. I carefully asked her what the book was about. I will never forget her reply: 'I will soon be seventy years old. It's time to prepare for my death. I don't have much, but if I die alone here in the mountains, I've written short messages for all my friends here. Buddha, Shiva, Mohammed or God willing, my lines will be passed on … I have also written some messages for you. It has been a wonderful time together and you have become a very special friend to me. Thank you for being here.'

I was shocked, and felt moved at the same time. I had never heard anyone speak so openly about death. It occurred to me that I was only a few years younger than Alexandra. But I still had so many plans to follow up on ... there were so much more that I wanted to see, so many more countries I wanted to travel to.

My ambitions and desires were those of a typical westerner: travelling, shopping, eating, drinking, sex, etc. Greed and addiction are what keep us going. Eternal restlessness and anxiety are the companions of our short lives, until it ends abruptly. This made me circle back to a thought that had been in my mind for a long time. Alexandra was the right person to talk to about it. The words slowly found a way to my lips. 'Alexandra, I too have thought about my death. Of course, I will be cremated, as is our custom. But every time I sit in this romantic cemetery in front of the church, I dream of being buried here. An urn with some of my ashes will do. Even after my death, I want to be able to look down on the shining golden roofs of the Dalai Lama's temple from this impressive place—just as I can now. Let us both find a common grave here ... I dream that one day my grandchildren will come and visit me here. They will inevitably have to come to terms with the culture and religion of my second home. Perhaps that would be a much better legacy than leaving behind money and property at a notary's office.'

We both looked at each other for a long time and nodded in silence. We both had long since realised that a person's true legacy had nothing to do with money or material possessions, for these were transient and therefore meaningless. What held value was the dharma, the path that each individual had walked in their current life—and that was the only true legacy that remained.

We sat for a long time, lost in thought, gazing out over the Kangra Valley far below, the golden roofs of the Dalai Lama's temple glistening in the setting sun.

A few months later I received an upsetting message: Alexandra had been admitted to Dr Barbara's hospital far down in the Kangra Valley with a serious, unexplained illness.

Around the same time, I received a text message from Jakob, a mutual friend who lived in the mountains above Dharamshala. He requested me to send some money to support the twenty-four-hour care being provided at Dr Barbara's hospital. The government hospitals were completely overcrowded and inaccessible due to the ongoing pandemic.

Of course, I also paid for a very expensive trip to Chandigarh, which was a seven-hour drive. It was the only way to ensure that Alexandra could be examined by MRI.

Unfortunately, after returning, Alexandra kept slipping into unexplained unconsciousness. Suddenly there was a big question mark over whether we would be able to fulfil our dream of having a common grave in the most beautiful place in the world.

24

Died of Heartbreak

I was lying by the pool of a luxury hotel in Dubai, writing the last chapters of my book. Blue skies, luxury everywhere. There was glitz and glamour around every corner, with countless luxury limousines parked outside the five-star hotel. The rich and famous enjoy their usual unimaginable prosperity being carefree and far removed from the real problems of society. The power of the sheikhs, and therefore the power of money, reigns in Dubai. It is not only European tourists who, as parasites of wealth, pour even more money into the already overflowing coffers. Greed and lust, shopping or sex, there is something for everyone's desires. But that's not what I was in the mood for. After eight months of lockdown during the pandemic, I escaped to get away from the unfriendly weather for a few days and finally finish my book.

The hotel I made a reservation at employed several Indian staff. This gave me a chance to talk to them about the current situation in their country. Coronavirus numbers were going through the roof in India. Hospitals and intensive care units were bursting at the seams. Oxygen tanks, essential for survival, were in short supply. They were being traded as if they were no less than gold.

India is one of the world's largest producers of medicines. Officials say millions of people have been vaccinated against coronavirus, and vaccines have been exported to some ninety-two countries around the world. According to media reports, this made India a model country for coronavirus immunisation. However, many people from often-inaccessible regions of the Himalayas and other overpopulated parts of India are still virtually unvaccinated. With mega events like Kumbh Mela in Prayagraj, which takes place every twelve years attracting millions of visitors, cases of coronavirus patients must have increased.

It is compulsory for every *yogi* (Indian saint) to attend the event. The subsequent bath in the holy Ganga promises to bring each of them a step closer to the paradise of Shiva. Mostly naked or wearing only a loincloth, they parade in groups of hundreds of thousands, walking on the banks of the Ganga. Even during the pandemic, these people flouted rules of lockdown, social distancing and even wearing face masks. Even though the government tried to contain the pandemic with measures that would be incomprehensible in our part of the world, their efforts were completely futile in front of old rituals and traditions. Of course, Covid-positive people were confined to their homes and to prevent them from going outside. One would find stamps on their hands, which would highlight that they were under home quarantine.

In another federal state, the authorities demanded selfies from households at regular intervals to prove that they were staying indoors and complying with the norms. But, as seen in supposedly progressive and capitalist Europe, there are also conspirators and opponents of the government. There are people who enjoy the benefits of democracy to the full but do not realise that this form of government only works well as long as every person backs it up. Never did it become so easy for the layman to see the power that dictatorial countries can exercise in such situations. Those violating the rules were punished draconically, with the state making use of the police and the military. China, the country of origin of the pandemic, was deemed to be effectively controlling the spread of the coronavirus, thanks to their restrictive measures. Apparently, their economy continued to flourish, while countless companies went bankrupt in our part of the world. However, as always, information from China should be taken with a pinch of salt.

Rightly, nobody would want to see such a despicable form of government become a reality in their own country. For more than seventy years, we have been used to having a say in the formation of government through the democratic election of our representatives. When a government makes decisions that we find unpalatable—as during the coronavirus crisis—we complain and criticise until another political party addresses our capitalist fears, or until we go to the ballot box again and the eternally dissatisfied voter gets another chance.

Never did one witness what democracy can achieve through a show of unity. As J.F. Kennedy said: 'Ask not what your country can do for you—ask what you can do for your country.'

No family, no business, no larger society can function without a leader supported by the people. The maintenance of public order is still best guaranteed by a democratically elected government. Even the great lamentations of the anti-vaccinationists and conspiracy theorists won't help.

Their alternative—if you come to think of it—would only be dictatorship. And anyone who goes through life with their eyes open should know what that would look like!

The powerful Sheikh Rashid Maktoum in Dubai, when asked how he saw the future of his country, replied: 'My grandfather rode a camel and my father did the same. I drive a Mercedes and my son drives a Land Rover. My grandson will probably have a big car too. But my great-grandson will probably go back to riding a camel. I also like to give reasons for this. There are a few principles that have always governed everything in life. To be more precise, prosperity in our country produces parasites, not survivors.'

What a wise statement by the Sheikh. He, who has made the desert state of Dubai one of the most economically successful countries even without black gold, has been working on attracting the parasites of wealth to his country to make it even richer. While we fall prey to addiction and dependency on drugs, alcohol, shopping and sex, Sheikh Rashid and many other able businessmen like him make a profit. But his and our grandchildren will eventually pay the price. However, power and dictatorship seem capable of prolonging this prosperity. Democracy and its parasitic prosperity, on the other hand, seem to have little chance.

The pandemic showed a glimpse of the future, obvious to those who pay attention. Our politicians are learning to lead the people through the most necessary measures. The police, the military and the authorities are demanding more power, which they are unlikely to relinquish. Governments have realised this, and the people have demanded it. As the ancient Romans said, 'You can't get rid of the ghosts you summon.' Neither Egypt, the empire of the pharaohs, nor ancient Greece, where democracy was born, nor the Roman Empire were wiped out in a final, devastating battle. In the end, it was always the much slower, creeping death of unchecked prosperity.

While I was chatting with the Indian waiters in Dubai about restaurant recommendations and the usual trivialities of a luxury holiday, I received a WhatsApp message from Jakob, my Austrian friend in the mountains above Dharamshala:

'Günter, I have some sad news. Alexandra, our dear friend, the one you always speak of so lovingly as "your Indian angel", is dying. She's been having epileptic seizures for days; she is not waking up. Dr Barbara has tried everything, she has phoned specialists all over the world, she has even consulted a local neurologist. We are at a loss. Thanks for your support. Two Tibetan nuns are looking after her round the clock. With your financial help, we were able to take her to the hospital in Chandigarh, six hours away, which is the only place in the area with an MRI facility. Thank God, she doesn't have cancer. Her brain should be fine too. Luckily, no visible disease was found.'

I was shocked! Alexandra was about seventy years old, but she always seemed to be in great health, always balanced and relaxed. She meditated daily and was a master of Tibetan medicine, the basic rules of which she practised extensively on herself. What could have gone wrong and made Alexandra, my angel, so ill? Far away from India, far away from my home in Austria, I thought about how I could help her. Dr Barbara, a Viennese doctor who has dedicated her life to helping people in need in a simple, donor-funded hospital near Dharamshala, was not available. I asked Christian, a very dear friend and experienced neurologist in my hometown of Linz, to contact her and come up with an advice together. He was also unable to reach Barbara on her phone. I informed Aditya, the maharaja. After all, his influence as the former ruler of the region was not insignificant. But he was also busy looking after his wife, who had contracted coronavirus. He wrote back to tell me that he was in constant contact with Dr Barbara, but because of the surge in Covid-positive cases, the government had forbidden people from leaving their houses, especially as another lockdown had been imposed.

When doctors are helpless, prayer is often the only thing that helps. I wrote to Nick, a mutual Tibetan friend of Alexandra and mine, to find out how they were doing. He too was in touch with Dr Barbara.

'We don't know what to do, we don't know how to help your angel Alexandra', such agonising messages were increasingly reaching me via WhatsApp in the far-off luxury of Dubai. How worthless all the splendour, all the money is when death comes round the corner. Alexandra probably knew a long time ago that this moment would come very soon. During our last personal conversation on the little bench outside St John in the Wilderness, she had already shown me her booklet of messages that she was preparing for her friends. She had already absorbed the message of her imminent death. But was this how she had imagined it? Alone, breathing her last in the mountains of the Himalayas? Probably, Alexandra wanted it that way. It made me think about the seriously ill people in our latitudes during the pandemic. They had to spend their final hours just as lonely and alone. How strange is the thought of falling asleep peacefully surrounded by loved ones. Indeed, most people quickly dismiss the idea of even thinking about their own death, even though it is inevitable.

Caregivers tell us time and again that the most common last words uttered by a dying person are: 'I wish I had done this or that.' By the time these words are uttered, of course it is too late.

I received a new WhatsApp message from Dr Barbara: 'A Tibetan nun has just come to see Alexandra. She is a very special woman who is in possession of very ancient secrets of Tibetan medicine. She also has the ability to see what is really wrong with a person's body ... The nun said that Alexandra was dying of a broken heart and that there was no medicine for an unbearable heartbreak.'

Perhaps, it was the unattainable love for our mutual friend, the Maharaja, whom she adored above all else and accompanied for many years in the shadow of his wedded wife. Or perhaps it was the Buddha's call for her to be reborn in a higher, better reincarnation ...

Alexandra, my angel, sleep well. We shall meet again, in a better world.

25

Shots Fired in the Himalayas

Brandl Bakery opened its renovated shop right across our restaurant. Nothing was spared. A beautiful counter made of polished dark granite invited all to buy the handmade specialities that were prepared in keeping with the old baker's tradition. A huge shelf filled with a wide variety of breads could be seen. Many of the 'rich and famous' had accepted the invitation of the 'master of handmade pastries' to pay their respects to the successful transformation. One thing was certain: every Saturday, there would be queues of people outside waiting to take home one of the coveted crispy delicacies. There would be endless speeches by politicians and chamber officials. The local media tried to capture all the flattering words with their cameras. The first guests started to eat from the sumptuous buffet. Wine, Prosecco and cold beer were served in abundance along with the delicious food. Everything was free, of course. There were VIPs everywhere indulging in small talk, trying to outdo each other with their smiles.

It all suggested that everything was going well, not just there but across the country.

Suddenly I felt my phone vibrate in my jacket's pocket. I immediately unlocked it to check the new email notification that had popped up. The subject line alone woke me up: 'Shots fired in the Himalayas'. Shocked, I hastily scanned the body of the email. I couldn't believe what I read next: Around eighty Tibetan children were said to have been chased across the Himalayas into Nepal and prevented from leaving the land occupied by the Chinese soldiers, with targeted shots. It was feared that they were killed!

The terrible news came from a Tibetan friend in exile who was undoubtedly trustworthy. For some time, he had been sending important information from his homeland to a central point in Europe, where the messages were translated into various national languages and then passed on. It was a set system that the Tibetans had been skilfully using for decades to draw the world's attention to acts of violence against their people. They also used it for disseminating information about the arrest of 'disobedient' Tibetans or about new intimidating regulations and laws of the Chinese occupiers. But now there were more and more reports of self-immolations by young monks who wanted to draw attention to the massive oppression they were being subjected to.

However, there has never been anything like this—the fatal shootings of children who wanted nothing more than being able to practise their culture in a foreign country while studying about Buddhism, close to their living god, the Dalai Lama.

I had lost my appetite for small talk. There were ongoing wars all over the world. The press was constantly reporting on IS terrorists in the Middle East; the war in Yemen with thousands dead; the war in Afghanistan with its American and NATO soldiers, sold to us as the supposed 'saviours of the world from the Taliban'; or dozens of theatres of war in Africa.

But no one in the world press was even remotely aware of the suffering of my Tibetan friends. The real reason for this has always remained a mystery to me. Who can blame them if many Tibetans are trying to escape the grip of the Chinese occupiers and flee to India, the largest democratic country in the world?

I had heard countless stories of Tibetan children's harrowing escapes, and their accounts of these traumatic experiences were always accompanied by violent bouts of crying. Most of them were children from my orphanages who had previously endured weeks of hardship to find a new, better future in a foreign country.

The farewell scenes when we had to part were always heartbreaking. They clung to me like burrs when the time came to say goodbye. 'Father Josef', that's what they often called me, 'Father Josef, please do come back, we need you so much', they begged. For the children, I had become part of their family, and this brought back memories, especially of the painful farewells to their families back home. I too often cried realising their longing for their home, which was so close and yet so far away.

My heart went out to them, especially when the housemothers of the many SOS Children's Villages on the border with China told me about the refugee children's recurring crying fits at night.

At first, I avoided writing down their stories when I decided to pen this book. At some point, however, I realised that my 'Tibetan Travelogues' would not be complete without the children's experiences, and that I would probably regret not having included them. I decided to include their experiences in my book, in their honour. So, I asked the children to write down about their journey of escaping across the snow-covered mountains of the Himalayas.

I also asked young artists from the Thangka Painting School to make me drawings depicting their journey. While the very artistic paintings were characterised by high mountains, snow and yaks, they also included scenes of pools of blood and dead people shot by Chinese soldiers with rifles.

After very frank discussions with the school management, I received their blessings. They had trust in me which was the result of a long-standing friendship.

Some of the children's essays spoke for themselves and did not need an additional explanation in order to be understood. One needn't be a psychologist to recognise their eternal trauma, something the children will carry within them for the rest of their lives.

I came across a hard evidence of another dangerous escape, and it confirmed that I had done the right thing. Bulgarian mountaineers had, for the first time, captured the gruesome act of bloodshed on video. The tragedy had occurred just a few days earlier on the endless white snowfield of the 5,716-metre-high Nangpa La, at the foot of the sacred Cho Oyu ('Turquoise Goddess') mountain, over which people have travelled to nearby Nepal since time immemorial.

Later, American Hollywood star Richard Gere, a long-time personal friend of the Dalai Lama, presented the same footage of the Bulgarian mountaineering team to the public at the Cinema for Peace gala in Berlin in 2006, but even after that the response from the press was limited.

It dawned on me how and why would anybody stand up to mighty China for a few dead children!

EPILOGUE

Between Dream and Reality: A Tibetan Fairy Tale

The word *kora* comes from Tibetan Buddhism. It means the circumambulation of a special, usually sacred place, such as a statue, a sacred tree, a lake, a mountain or a temple. It roughly corresponds to the name of our pilgrimage routes to the holy sites in Europe. The exact origin of this name is unclear and may be hidden in the depths of ancient history. The fact is, however, that these 'circumambulations of holy places' can be found in almost all religions.

Probably the most important and powerful kora in Buddhism is the 53-kilometre circumambulation of the sacred Mount Kailash in the trans-Himalayas. Pilgrims walk around the sacred mountain at an altitude of 5,700 metres. After 108 circumambulations (!), one is said to attain enlightenment (strangely enough, this is the same number as the beads in our rosaries). Thousands of pilgrims following Tibetan Buddhism, Hinduism, Jainism and the ancient Bon religion endure endless hardship and privation, even death. Year after year, this kora takes its toll on pilgrims. Time and time again, people die on this journey, from cold, exhaustion or altitude sickness. I had often planned to go on this very special pilgrimage, but somehow it never materialised, and perhaps it was for the best.

I decide to go on a different kora. It was the Dalai Lama's temple in Dharamshala—an easy, 2-kilometre long but wonderfully romantic path with fantastic views, deep into the fertile Kangra plains. The snow-capped 6,000-metre peaks of the Dhauladhar range gleamed from the top, with the Tibetan highlands and China beyond.

It was late afternoon, just before the 'blue' hour, when the sun hits the Himalayan foothills at a very favourable angle—the ideal time to take beautiful photographs. The normally dusty air near the busy roads appeared to be clear and sparkling, and the subtleties of its radiance resembled the glow of an emerald. It was a time for dreamers and romantics, for peace and meditation. Even the countless colourful birds seemed to have taken a break at this special hour.

Two cows greeted me at the entrance to the narrow path. With their long tails, they chased away the many mosquitoes that were buzzing around their sweaty bodies. Hungrily, they opened their slimy mouths but I had no bread to feed them. I was embarrassed and felt apologetic from within. I quickened my pace along the winding path and finally disappeared into the shade of the huge cedar trees that surrounded the Dalai Lama's temple and living quarters. When I turned around, I could see the cows still looking in my direction. To me, they looked disappointed. They had certainly not accepted my apology and thus my guilty conscience worsened.

The pilgrimage routes in the Himalayas are marked by countless offerings from pilgrims, most of whom travel from far and wide. Colourful prayer flags hung on the mighty trees rustle at the edge of the path, carrying the printed mantras into the vast blue sky, supported by the winds rising from the Kangra Valley. Thousands of pilgrims leave these prayer flags on trees to pray for a path to a better world, a higher rebirth. The eternal wind is said to carry the inscribed mantras down into the vastness of the Kangra Valley. The sound created by the fluttering of the colourful scraps of cloth is like the symphony of a very special orchestra. Endless, metre-high walls of mani stones, colourfully painted with the mantra '*Om mani padme hum*', silently point the way along the narrow path. I could see some of the huge prayer wheels, lined like silent sentinels, still rotating after being turned by the pilgrims.

It was a place suitable for dreamers and meditators. One would rarely see groups of people around in the area. The pilgrimage is to be undertaken alone. It is about the time after one has left a place and is yet to reach another. The journey becomes the goal. Those who do not move do not change and remain eternally distant from the happiness of nirvana. It is a path that I have followed again and again—a path into the unknown. Only the seeker and the determined dare to tread this difficult path leading to their innermost being, for it is also the path of change accompanying as an invisible companion and also as the guardian of your soul. The same questions surfaces in my mind time and again: 'Why can't I achieve this inner contemplation at home in the West?'

I have repeatedly come across sacred cows silently following my path as if they had been chosen by a higher power to show me the way.

It was time for me to meditate my own way. As I continued my trek, I could slowly feel getting drawn to a dreamlike state of infinite emptiness. Then a feeling of happiness and freedom overpowered me. It felt as if I had finally arrived at my 'new home'. I was feeling increasingly satisfied. My steps slowed down and I started moving as if in a trance. Completely new, unknown or deeply hidden thoughts were now surfacing in my mind, and that could only mean one thing: I was once one of them, and that is why I was feeling 'at home'.

At the turn of the path, I noticed an old pilgrim sitting on one of the benches weathered by the monsoon rains. Using the fingers of his right hand, he signalled me to join him. Before taking my seat, I studied his face. His eyes were almost closed and he looked up at the sky like a blind man with his head slightly raised. His eyes, slightly opened, reminded me of a snake for he had slightly greenish cornea. He seemed to be sitting in a meditative pose. A long, weathered stick was lying beside him. While I was busy studying the man, with a slight movement of his wrinkled fingers, he suggested that I sit next to him.

We sat quietly side by side for a long time. Suddenly, I felt a strange but very pleasant energy emanating from his body, first scanning and then completely enveloping me. Then he started to communicate. I couldn't understand the language he was speaking in, but I felt he was speaking to me. It was a strange, gentle mixture of soft tones mixed with foreign dialects. After not being able to notice even a slight movement of his body, I tried to follow his words. He might have been mumbling to himself. Suddenly, he stood up and raised his hands, as if in defence, and roared: 'Tiger, tiger, tiger.' He went on repeating the words loudly. He seemed to be frightened as if he was being attacked by an imaginary animal.

I jumped out of fear. I looked around, completely unsettled. No tiger sightings had been reported in the area for centuries! In the past, I have seen these mighty predators in faraway national parks in India, for it is there and only there where these true rulers of the jungle still live, protected by rangers. If not tigers, hungry leopards must have been spotted, even if only occasionally, sneaking into the villages at the foothills of the Himalayas during night.

I hope there were no tigers in the area. I was worried thinking about the old man. Meanwhile, he jumped, as if in a trance, and continued to fight against a creature invisible to me. He was still swinging his sturdy cane wildly, while I had taken refuge on a large rock nearby to stay safe. From up there, I took a closer look at the surroundings and finally made sure that there were no tigers around.

Finally, the old man seemed to come out of his trance and looked at me as I stood on the rock, feeling anxious and unsure. He began to laugh out loud. His skin, which seemed to somehow have a dark green tint, returned to the lighter tone it had been before. He held out his hands to help me and indicated that I should climb down from my seemingly safe 'lookout'. Frightened, but following his reassuring voice, I climbed down from the rock, and once again his pointing fingers suggested that I take a seat beside him. He looked at me briefly, scrutinised me, and then fell into another trance.

This time, without looking at me, he started narrating a story in a language that seemed to me a concoction of many. Once again, his eyes closed a little more than halfway, and the remainder of his eyes were covered by green snake-like skin. He was one of the mysterious Tibetan oracles said to exist in the endless valleys of the Himalayas. I hoped to be able to grasp the essence of his story.

'She is a tigress, a very powerful tigress,' he mumbled to himself. 'She was once the queen of the jungle—invincible and feared. There are countless stories about this feline predator, though it is said that no human has ever set eyes on her. Today, however, she has become a metaphor in countless Indian–Tibetan stories passed down from family to family in the Himalayas for generations. I have just seen it again. It has haunted me for many lifetimes. Ask about the story of the "tigress and the goat" and you will understand what I mean.'

He stood up, straightened his dirty skirt, and looked me deep in the eyes as he bid adieu. He turned around without a word and disappeared among the prayer flags and mani stones.

I sat there, not knowing whether all of that was part of a dream or my meditative state of mind. Perplexed, I scanned the area for the dreaded predator. There was none, and the old yogi too had disappeared.

It was already dawn; the blue hour was drawing to a close. Slowly, I got up. My mind was racing with questions and, lost in thought, I walked down the rest of the kora to the great gate that led to the Dalai Lama's temple.

Only the honking and rattling of the countless taxis and buses could pull me out of my reverie. I was back. Was it all just a dream? Did I really experience everything? Struggling under the weight of the unanswered questions, I walked to the guest room in the house of the Maharaja of Kangra, the house of my friend Aditya Katoch. I wanted to share with him about what had happened. It was only him who could help me clear my confusion. I wondered whether he would also be able to explain the deeper meaning of my experience—if there was one?

So, if anyone could explain the strange experience at the kora, it was my friend, the Maharaja. Aditya is well known for his deep knowledge of the history of his country and his ancestors, hence I was sure he would tell me more about the 'Tale of the Tigress'. I had sent in a word to have a chat with him. A short time later, he was waiting for me in his guest room.

He gestured for me to sit next to him. On the wall behind him hung the skin of a mountain leopard, shot by his father decades ago, he assured me. The bar was open as usual. He offered me a drink of my choice. I opted for a whisky mixed with plenty of soda, and sat down next to him. Then I took a deep breath before launching into a torrent of stories. Once I had shared the complete incident with Aditya, he smiled meaningfully, which of course added to my excitement. Then he furrowed his brow and enquired about the appearance of the old man's long stick. Lost in a thought, he took several puffs on his thick Gurkha cigar and muttered 'Milarepa'.

I was familiar with the word, but I wanted to be sure and asked, 'What did you say? Milarepa?'

Aditya looked deep into my eyes. 'Yes, you met Milarepa!'

I started to stammer: 'What, me? The Milarepa?'

Aditya simply nodded. He had managed to hide his excitement well so far, but the previously pleasurable puffs on his cigar were starting to give way to frantic puffs. Speechless myself, I lit a cigar, took a deep breath and took deep puffs, sitting inside the small room.

In Tibetan–Indian mythology, Milarepa is regarded as the greatest magician, philosopher as well as a saint. He is revered as a model of hard work, diligence and faith, and his poems and songs have been passed down to us in countless forms. Coming across an apparition of Milarepa is considered a great blessing. Those, in front of whom he appears, are spared a low rebirth.

'To meet Milarepa is something great, something auspicious and something very special,' my friend began to explain.

'So, did I see him or did he appear to me?' I asked.

Aditya nodded again as if it were the most natural thing to do in the world. Not daring to think about it, I instead asked about the tigress story.

'Every child here in the Himalayas knows the tale of the tigress and Milarepa, who appears in the form of a goat, my friend,' Aditya continued. 'But the tale is actually one of the many metaphors for the countless great love stories in our country. They are all about an infinitely great love, a love that was never allowed to be fulfilled due to various influences, such as a traditionally upheld social order. This often saw tragic consequences. A long time ago, I myself fell victim to such a great love, simply because of my background and position.'

As he began to recount his own love story, he turned his head slightly and raised his eyes lovingly to the infinite, falling back on burgeoning memory. The smile that appeared on his face remained for a little while.

'Franziska was a beautiful girl. I met her in Munich, and we had a wonderful time together. She was one of the countless hippie girls of the 1960s, but for me she was by far the prettiest and smartest of them all. I had the best time of my life with her. She loved me and I loved her. I wanted nothing more than to marry her and have children with her.'

I could sense that he was about to reveal another of his wonderful stories from an eventful life.

'You see,' Aditya continued, 'my father was much more powerful than me. He was a real maharaja—a maharaja with power, a lot of power. At the beginning of the twentieth century, he decided to build a huge dam up here in the Himalayas. The cities below the kingdom in the Rajasthan desert were extremely water-stressed, and the population was suffering massively from a water shortage that threatened their very existence. Irrigating the desert was the most ambitious goal imaginable up here, and it became the goal of his life. Together with the Maharaja of Jodhpur, he developed this huge water project and had a canal dug more than a thousand kilometres to the distant desert city of Rajasthan to finally supply Jodhpur with the water it needed to survive.

'In gratitude and recognition for this huge project, the Maharaja of Jodhpur promised my father his daughter Chandresh as my future wife. This had very complicated consequences. Not only did my love for Franziska stand in the way of this promise, but Chandresh was also madly in love with a Nepalese prince. It was as hopeless as a Greek tragedy, because in those days it was impossible to go against what our fathers had mutually agreed on. It was irrevocable—we both had to obey what our fathers had decided for us.'

At these last words, the wistful smile disappeared from Aditya's face, giving way to an expression of great regret. After a thoughtful pause, probably no longer than a few seconds, he continued in his usual calm tone.

'I have been married for over fifty years. You can certainly see us both as victims of the concept of arranged marriage that is still a common practice today. But like everything in life, there was a silver lining. My wife was later appointed minister for women's rights and, because of her personal experience, she has been very active in the abolition of such forced marriages. She was able to at least stir a change. However, India's culture is thousands of years old and wouldn't shed its skin as easily as a snake.'

Aditya paused again before drawing a direct comparison with Europe: 'Basically, with all these arranged marriages, it's no different here.'

Probably noticing the incredulous expression on my face, he explained his train of thought with two plausible examples. 'The emperors and kings of your huge Habsburg empire created a world empire in this way, and every wealthy father of a peasant's daughter will try to increase his landholdings by finding a suitable boy from an equally large neighbour, won't he?'

He continued impassively: 'I understand that in Europe you have a divorce rate of about 50 per cent. Here it's not even five! Believe me, at first glance, the women here don't seem to have as many rights. Yet, in many ways, they are happier and more content than the women there. Women here have a dignity and grandeur not found in your latitudes. Love is not always our priority, because there are values that are more important to us: security of the family, feeding the children, caring for the elderly, supporting the village community, passing on culture and traditions are our top priorities.'

He paused for a single but a very deep breath before continuing.

'You have lost many of these treasures that are so important to us, even within your families. You are organised by the state and financially secure. But in return you have to work more and more and pay more and more taxes. Even your wives are already trapped in this hamster wheel of the diabolical cycle. When you don't know what to do, you vote for another new government, which promises you gifts that you will have to pay back for in the form of new taxes. Any form of coexistence ultimately needs someone to make decisions. In ancient India, it was usually the strongest, the most powerful. In our case, it was my father, the maharaja!'

Aditya was now in full swing, and a broad smile returned on his face as he added with a mischievous look: 'Well, the cleverness mostly came from the women as advisers in the background!'

But he was yet to reach the end of his argument.

'If the king's decisions were not good for the people, his followers would simply desert him. I know what I'm talking about ... don't forget you're talking to the head of one of the oldest clans in the world. After all, he had a few thousand years of experience behind him—both good and bad!'

Inwardly, I agreed with him. The often misunderstood European freedom, the call for emancipation and the right to freedom of expression forced us to give up many valuable traditions. Democracy, in my opinion, is when a representative is elected by a majority. But that representative should be supported accordingly. Constant rejection of governments because they make unpleasant laws or regulations, and emergence of ever new smaller parties do more harm than good to our country, our culture and our communities. The current situation in the West corresponds to the permanent dissatisfaction and insecurity of our fellow human beings. It is supported and caused by the enormous wealth created by our fathers and mothers. But, as everyone can see, it is rapidly diminishing. I even dare to predict the beginning of the decline of our powerful community and European culture. The West is already badly infected by the insidious disease of affluence, and we are all spreading the very 'virus' with frightening rapidity. We are not prepared to build up enough 'antibodies' to preserve the heritage created by generations before us. The ruthless pursuit of wealth and prosperity has spread through our society beyond morality and social behaviour.

Such behaviour is alien to the Buddhist faith. Those who have a lot of money are not to be considered rich. The truly rich are those who are content and have chosen the path to happiness. The trust and support of a democratically elected government, which as servants of the people must support this path, is a prerequisite for passing on this legacy to our children.

Bhutan is probably the only country in the world that has enshrined happiness as a way of life, acknowledging it as a vital index in its constitution. We urgently need to do the same, but I fear that this pious wish will unfortunately go unheard.

Aditya watched me as I slipped into deep thoughts. He knew I agreed with him on many things. After spending more than a quarter of a century as a permanent guest in his country, I have come to question many things in his world and do not always see our much-vaunted Western achievements as progress.

Somewhat startled by the deviations in our conversation, I took a strong sip of whisky and asked Aditya to finally tell me about the tale of the tigress.

'Have you read about Osho?' he asked me. 'This great Indian philosopher of our country emphasises in his works and lectures the importance of meditation, mindfulness, love, courage and humour. These are all qualities that he describes as psychologically repressed. Many of our innate feelings or emotions have been lost, especially due to the constant demand to subordinate religious traditions to political socialisation. Osho's complete works are rightly in the library of the Indian Parliament alongside those of Gandhi.

'In the very first pages of his book, he contradicts your Sigmund Freud, probably the most influential Western thinker and psychologist of the twentieth century. Freud claimed that human beings are born neurological. Osho, on the other hand, sees it differently. People are born naturally and in reality. But the neurosis is already at work at the moment of birth. You are not one, you are two or even many people. The humanity that surrounds you drives you towards neurosis even as a child. You are born as one who feels, and that is exactly what is taken away from you. You are taught to suppress your feelings and replace them with thinking. This is where the splitting of a person's true personality begins in the so-called civilised world.

'If a child wants to cry, he's not allowed to because his parents don't approve. He is forced to "behave" properly. Only then will he be loved. It is not easy for a child to receive love, because he has to obey certain rules, even if they contradict his childlike nature. This way of thinking is constantly imposed on him. He gradually forgets his original nature.

'This is how the core of your sentient heart then resembles a dormant volcano, consisting mostly of magma remnants. The icy armour of everyday life freezes it over the course of life. The all-feeling heart still has needs for love, for example, and this is when the split personality, which has developed over the years, begins to think, weigh, categorise, control and seduce. Add to this the fear of failure or disappointment. Your increasingly powerful personality takes over and you become an ice king or ice princess. Even for basic needs, such as to be loved and acknowledged, performing well in life becomes paramount. The capitalist world is full of such split personalities and does not stop at the movers and shakers of big politics. Even the young boardrooms are full of these split personalities. Therefore it is not surprising that many of these insecure people are looking for a way back here in distant Tibet, a way back to the roots of their original nature,' Aditya looked at me with a smile and added, 'just like you, my friend.'

He paused for a moment as he explained Osho's philosophy. It was a magical moment, because the Maharaja seemed to be able to sense my innermost thoughts. He then continued: 'Aren't you too someone who is looking for this way back to his past? I've known you for almost fifteen years now. That's a long time, and I've observed you a lot. I now know that in your past life you were one of us, for sure! How else do you explain your deep connection with the Himalayas? I just don't know if you were a Tibetan monk or an Indian yogi!'

Aditya began to laugh as he said this. The laughter began faintly, then became loud, and then culminated in a furious fit of laughter, making it difficult for me to filter out his words in his stream of words. But the bottom line was that I was probably a loner like Milarepa, someone who tried to practice both religions, and that I was a lonely snow leopard who has found his way back home ... how beautiful!

Aditya's laughter was contagious. When the urge to laugh along subsided a little, I expressed a wish to return to the subject.

'What about the story of the tigress?' I admonished Aditya and added, 'Your stories are incredibly exciting, but what about the tigress?' I eagerly pushed for the beginning of the conversation I wanted to have.

'Well,' Aditya began, 'as I said, it's a metaphor for everything we've discussed so far. Just like your Western fairy tales, it starts with "once upon a time" and goes like this: Milarepa lived in the form of an old, wise goat in a Tibetan mountainous village in the densely forested foothills of the Himalayas. At the same time, a feared tigress lived in the dark neighbouring jungle. She regularly came to the small village to kill water buffaloes, goats, sheep and dogs. Milarepa, the great Buddhist magician, was asked by the villagers to help them fight the dreaded feline predator in the form of a goat. Of course, the "goat" knew that he was a tasty treat for the tigress; so with some trepidation, he set off into the depths of the jungle to find the big cat.

'With some difficulty, he reached a cave on a distant hill. The view from there was breathtaking, even for him. A blue river shone in the distance on the seemingly endless horizon. It was late, and the goat was fascinated by the sunset on the horizon.

'The tigress, on the other hand, had her eye on him as she could look down into the valley and keep a close watch on everything that was going on. While he was still mesmerised by the uniqueness of the cave and its impressive surroundings, the goat suddenly heard the tigress's voice. She was sitting nearby, well camouflaged on a rock, and seemed to have been watching the goat all the time.

'"Hello, you old goat," she called to him, slightly smug. "Are you lost, or just looking for a place to spend the night?" The goat was startled as the tigress brushed her snow-white whiskers with her huge paws. It looked as if she was in two minds about whether to eat the goat for dinner or breakfast.

'But Milarepa was wise and experienced. Seeing the fresh bones in front of the entrance of the cave, he immediately realised that the beast had already devoured its dinner. So it was the right time to engage the queen of the jungle in a conversation. Perhaps he could persuade her to stop visiting the small village without a fight and spare the many vital animals there.

'The two rivals studied each other for a long time. Milarepa noticed how the tigress had changed her appearance. No other tigress was like her and no male tiger had ever been good enough for her to mate with. None could meet her demands and so she preferred her life of solitude.

'Milarepa watched with interest as the tigress searched his eyes for any signs of fear and anxiety. Lifting her head slightly, she showed her huge white fangs. But now that she could see no indications of dread in her seemingly secure prey, she began to circle him. She showed off her muscles and her dangerous claws. Her fur shone golden with a black veil in the evening light, and she lifted her long tail seductively, moving it back and forth in a slow pendulum rhythm, first to hypnotise the goat and then to bite him such that all his warm blood would drain away. Only then would she begin to eat the best parts ... It was a pity she had already eaten a young springbok for dinner. On closer inspection, however, the old goat didn't look too bad, and he was probably experienced and brave too. Perhaps there would be some interesting conversation before she ate him? Something different from the eternal chatter of the young tigers.

'The billy goat also seemed to take a liking to the tigress. Forgetting the danger lurking in front of him, he scrutinised her very closely. Predator and prey suddenly forgot their innate needs and opened their hearts to one another. Soon they had forgotten that they were enemies because of their common interests. Even the great wizard Milarepa became so interested in talking to the tigress that he lost sight of his original mission.

'The tigress and the goat sat together all night, telling each other hundreds of wonderful stories from their lives. Fear turned to interest, interest turned to mutual admiration. The tigress admired the old goat's character and had to admit that she envied him for it. Soon the admiration grew into something like a seed of love.

'But morning came, and thoughts of the rules imposed on them since birth began to dominate the pace of events. Milarepa saw a tear in the tigress's beautiful brown eyes. Deep within, he realised that he had to return to his own ancestral world. The tigress felt the same. Suddenly, she rose to a majestic height, flexing all her muscles and claws and opening her mouth so wide that you could see her terrible fangs. A desperate, blood-curdling, long roar filled the jungle. With tear-filled eyes, she looked pleadingly into the eyes of her opponent. "Go," she said, "go quickly, before I have to follow the rules—I'm powerless against those!"'

Aditya looked at me exhausted, small beads of sweat spread across his forehead. Finally he blurted out, 'I too was a goat who met a tigress. But I, too, my friend, like many before me, had to obey the rules of my tradition. What remains is pain, a beautiful pain. I never want to lose it, because it is my memory of a volcano that has not been extinguished and is still seething inside me! What should not be, must not be. This is an unwritten law of our society. The rules we have been taught since birth devour our feelings and sometimes turn us into ice-cold zombies, just as Osho wrote!

'Each one of us has similar memories. You can try to forget them. If you don't succeed, if you can't forget, you must get rid of the burden. And then you must set out on the path and search for happiness. It's never too late.

'But please don't ask me why Milarepa wanted me to tell you about this metaphor, you have to find that out for yourself … look within yourself, you will only find the answer within yourself, try meditation. Search for happiness. It is at home here in the Himalayas. You are closer than you think. Maybe the old monk will come and give you some more tips,' Aditya added with a laugh.

It was getting late and now it was time to go to bed. Will the green-skinned old wise man visit me again in my dreams?

Glossary

Alexander the Great: A gruelling battle against the Indian king Porus took place on the Hydaspes River in 326 BC. Porus's troops were vastly outnumbered by Alexander's, but Porus relied on his foreign troops to fight him, firing spears and arrows from war elephants. Despite heavy losses to Alexander's army, Porus was defeated. By that time, the troops had marched some 18,000 kilometres. Their progress was slowed down by the incessant rain, and the soldiers marched on under inhuman conditions. Their clothes and boots were torn and constantly soaked, their food was spoiled, and their weapons, horses and wagons had become unusable. The strange weather, the hardships of the march and the endless, unconquerable vastness of India undermined their morale. Finally discouraged, the soldiers mutinied, forcing Alexander to turn back in 325 BC.

Bodhisattvas: In simple terms, they can be described as beings or deities who have attained enlightenment and then reincarnate of their own free will and compassion to help subsequent humanity attain enlightenment, to become one with God. In doing so, they give up the opportunity to enter the final liberation, the dissolution into the Absolute. Bodhisattvas are like Catholic guardian angels.

Earl of Elgin: James Bruce, the eighth Earl of Elgin and twelfth Earl of Kincardine (b. 20 July 1811 in London; d. 20 November 1863 in Dharamshala) was a British colonial official and diplomat. He was governor of Jamaica, Governor General of British North America and viceroy of India.

Gelug school: Out of the four main schools of Tibetan Buddhism, this is the newest Monastic tradition that spread in Tibet from the fifteenth century onwards.

Je Tsongkhapa Lobsang Dragpa (1357–1419): 'The Man from the Onion Valley' was a great reformer whose teachings later gave rise to the Gelug school of Tibetan Buddhism.

Khata: It is a traditional greeting shawl, usually made of white silk in Tibet, symbolising the pure heart of the person presenting it.

Kumbh Mela: The festival has been celebrated since ancient times, but the first written mention of it is found in the records of the Chinese traveller Xuanzang in the seventh century, who accompanied the ruler Harsha Vardhana to Prayag for the Kumbh Mela in AD 644. He observed Hindus as well as Buddhists and Jain monks at Triveni. The next mention of him was in 1822 by Bahadur Singh Bhatnagar, when the Kumbh Mela remained half empty due to a pilgrimage tax. In 2017, the Kumbh Mela was inscribed on UNESCO's Representative List of the Intangible Cultural Heritage of Humanity.

Kullu Valley: The fertile valley stretches from Mandi to the Rohtang Pass, rising slowly from 760 to 3,915 metres. In the south, it is only slightly wider than its steeply sloping gorge, where the Beas River sometimes meanders almost 300 metres below the narrow road.

Ladakh: It became a Union Territory of India on

31 October 2019. Previously, it was a division under the Indian state of Jammu and Kashmir, covering almost forty per cent of its area. Ladakh consists of the districts of Kargil and Leh. The region is largely mountainous and sparsely populated with 274,289 inhabitants in 2011. Known for the beauty of its remote mountains and Tibetan Buddhist culture, Ladakh is also known as Little Tibet.

Manali: It literally translates to 'home of Manu'. Manu was a mythical king. Legend has it that he survived the great flood that destroyed the world. According to one version, his ark—similar to that of Moses—landed near Manali after the flood, and Manu became the forefather of mankind. The Manali region is considered sacred, and Hindus make pilgrimages from far and wide to its holy sites, especially the temple complex of Goddess Hidimba Devi in the thousand-year-old cedar forest of Dhungri. Manali is the starting point of an ancient trade route to Ladakh, which continues via the Karakoram Pass to Yarkant and Khotan in the Tarim Basin. Today, the strategically significant national route to Ladakh (also known as the 'Manali–Leh Road') begins in Manali.

Mandi: It is a town in the Indian state of Himachal Pradesh. It is the administrative centre of the district of the same name.

Nyingmapa: It is the 'school of the ancients'. The so-called Red Hats are the oldest Tibetan Buddhist schools.

Om mani padme hum: It means 'O Jewel in the Lotus Flower', and is the universal mantra of love and compassion.

Polyandry: The word has its origin in the ancient Greek terms 'polys' meaning 'much' and 'aner' meaning 'man'. Thus it means many-manned.

Puja: It roughly translates to 'worship', similar to the Catholic Mass.

Rinpoche: It is a Tibetan term meaning 'precious one'. This title is applied at the end of the teacher's name, usually one who has been recognised as the reincarnation of a great teacher.

Rohtang Pass: It is a strategically important mountain pass in northern India in the interior of the Himalayas. Located in the state of Himachal Pradesh, it connects the upper valley of the Beas River in the south (Kullu Valley) with that of the Chandra River, a tributary of the Chenab, in the north. The recorded altitude of the pass is 3,978 metres above sea level and it lies about fifty kilometres north-east of the town of Manali. It is crossed by a national highway, which is only open during the summer months and links the north-western Indian state of Punjab with the mountain (and border) region of Ladakh. The pass is both a climatic and a cultural divide; it separates the wetter, monsoon-influenced, Hindu regions of the hills and midlands from the Buddhist-influenced, desert-like high mountains of the Himalayas. In October 2020, after more than ten years of construction, the 9-kilometre-long, two-lane Rohtang Tunnel (also known as the Atal Tunnel) was opened.

Sherabling Monastery: The monastery comprises 250 monks' quarters housing over 500 monks, three shrine halls and six shrine rooms.

Acknowledgements

I would like to dedicate this book above all to those who have made it possible for me to experience and share these wonderful impressions in the distant Himalayas, thousands of kilometres away from my restaurant.

I would particularly like to thank my wife Monika, my son Andreas, and our staff who ensured that my restaurant continues to flourish in my absence!

But most of all, I dedicate this book to the children of my Tibetan orphanages, to the carertakers and managers of the SOS-run Tibetan Children's Villages, and to my many Tibetan and Indian friends for their warm, everlasting hospitality and love.

Thanks are also due to my guests, friends and sponsors, especially the Kiwanis Club Linz and Kepler, whose support made many projects for my Tibetan friends possible!

I would especially like to thank my long-time friend Raja Shri Aditya Dev Chandra Katoch, the maharaja of Kangra, and his wonderful wife Chandresh Kumari Katoch, former Indian minister of culture, through whose friendship I was able to gain so much insight into the Indian high nobility.

Thanks to my Dutch angel Alexandra Reelick, whose many years of residence in her second home in India gave me remarkable insights into the secrets of Indian culture and Tibetan medicine. Sadly, she passed away before my book was published as a result of the terrible coronavirus pandemic outbreak. I would also like to thank my Tibetan friend of many years, Ngodup Wangdoo, who unfortunately also died of coronavirus before the book was completed.

Many thanks to the Austrian trade delegate in India, Hans-Jörg Hörtnagl, whose many years of experience in India meant that he was always able to provide me with important information.

Thanks also to my friend Gerd J. Schneeweis from Linz who, as an experienced author, was a great help to me in writing this book with many tips and advices.

I would also like to thank my long-time Tibetan friend and Buddhist monk Rigo Tulku Rinpoche for the many enlightening conversations. I am also grateful to our Tibetan godchild Sonam for the interesting stories about his training at the Tibetan medical monastery Men-Tsee-Khang and his time in the Himalayas.

A big thank you to my experienced Indian guide and long time friend Mohit Sharma and his wonderful wife Seema for always welcoming me into their family in Shimla. Thank you for showing me the beauties of your wonderful homeland and introducing me to the infinite secrets of Indian mysticism. Thank you, Mohit, for allowing me to travel many thousand miles with you over the past twenty-five years on some of the most dangerous terrains in the Himalayas, and for always bringing me safely to my destination.

My special thanks to His Holiness the Dalai Lama for the touching foreword and the many personal conversations over the twenty years of our acquaintance, which have given me the joy and energy to write this book!

Tashi Delek, namaste and thank you!